Ten

Cliff McCabe was born in   )61,
the fifth surviving child of what would become a family of eight
siblings. His formative years were spent in Cessnock, the main
backdrop for *Ten's a Crowd*. After marrying, he spent the next
sixteen years in Pollokshields before moving out of the city to
Kirkintilloch, where he now lives.

He married Eileen Patricia Keenan 1980 and they have two
ons, Paul and Clifford, who, with partners Alison and Pauline
ve produced four beautiful grandchildren: Connor, Jon Paul,
elsy and Sean.

Cliff stared writing after reading a best-seller and thinking that
e could do better. Whether he has or not, he says will leave for
others to judge. But he has loved trying.

The series *Ten's a Crowd* was written one chapter at a time for his
wife to read. Those chapters were passed on to family and then to
friends. Fed up with printing so many copies at home he published
his work in e-book format and they became local best-sellers. And
now, for the first time, *Ten's a Crowd* is published in paperback.

L
na

"The banter is brill. A must read."

"So true about Glasgow family life"

"Glaswegians will love it"

"Great wee story"

"FULL OF GLASGOW WIT AND CHARM"

"What a great read"

"A must-read"

"Such a fantastic writer"

"Leaves me wanting more"

"Unputdownable"

"Never want this story to end"

"KEPT ME UP ALL NIGHT"

"Would definitely recommend it"

"Well observed and very funny"

"Fab, fab, fabulous"

"Transports me back to my childhood"

"Can't wait for next book"

"What a great read. True to life and very funny"

"TOTALLY HILARIOUS"

"Brought back happy memories"

"AMAZING"

"Loved, loved, loved this book"

"Enjoyed all five"

"Can't wait for number six"

"Very funny and true to life"

"A fabulous collection"

"I feel as if I've grown up with the characters"

"GREAT BOOKS, GREAT STORIES"

"Fantastic story from Glasgow"

"Thanks Cliff for another great chapter in the lives of Danny and co"

"I felt as if I was part of the book. It really draws you in."

"I feel as though I'm part of their family. Can't wait for the next book. Love it."

"Each one had me on the edge of the chair waiting for the next one. This one made me laugh, made me cry and waiting to see where the family go from here."

"They're brilliant, sad, funny and most of all lovely memories of a proper close-knit family."

"Excellent. I hope the author writes more books."

"Fantastic and captivating. I enjoyed it and recommend to others"

"Very funny. Typical of its time"

"Hilarious account of a typical Glasgow family in the Seventies"

"Found myself crying with laughter at some of their antics."

"Glaswegians will love it and laugh so much."

"WOULD DEFINITELY RECOMMEND IT"

"Found it so down to earth. Glaswegians at their best"

"FIVE STARS FOR A GREAT BOOK."

"Can't wait for number six to come out"

Ten's a Crowd

The Heartwarming Story
of a Glasgow Family

(PART ONE)

Cliff McCabe

Fort Publishing Ltd

First published in 2015 by Fort Publishing Ltd, Old Belmont House,
12 Robsland Avenue, Ayr, KA7 2RW

Printed by Bell and Bain Ltd, Glasgow

Typeset by 3btype.com

Graphic design by Mark Blackadder

Front-cover illustration by Andy Bridge

ISBN: 978-1905769-49-0

This book is dedicated to my eternally beautiful wife,
Eileen,
for daring me to try and pushing me to succeed.

Author's Note

Glasgow 1960. I came kicking and screaming into existence. The fifth child of David and Margaret McCallister. They would go on to produce another three, providing me with the title of this book: eight children and two parents makes ten in total. But as the sum of the parts was greater than the individuals this often made ten seem like fifty. Trust me, I know what I am talking about when I say ten's a crowd; ten, in fact, is a multitude.

We were poor, not when-will-we-ever-eat-again poor, but my recollection is that I never wore a single piece of outer clothing that hadn't belonged to someone else first, unless my mother or one of my sisters had knitted it. However, whenever I mentioned this recollection to either of my parents or to my older siblings they would say it was nonsense. Yes we wore hand-me-downs but no more so than all the other large families in our area. Their recollection is that we did okay in comparison to the vast majority of our friends and neighbours.

No matter, the point of this tale is not that we were poor. Everybody was poor in one way or another; everybody was short of money. That was the norm. But some people also lacked morals, sympathy and the milk of human kindness. I hope that we didn't, I hope the point is that we rose above our circumstances and lived and died with our pride intact, a smile on our face or a tear in our eye. I can't be the judge of that. I am biased, but you can, if you are so inclined.

This isn't a rags-to-riches fairy-tale of poor boy or girl rising to great heights. We weren't extraordinary. None of us became prime minister or walked on the moon or even became famous outside of our own circle. But we lived full lives with a tremendous passion and energy, qualities instilled in us by our mother. Not a day of my life passed when she didn't tell me I was special, wonderful and god's gift to the world. In her eyes that was true of all her children, and we believed her. My siblings and I did without many things as we grew up but what we didn't go without was love, self-belief and a sense of family that was rock solid.

That was never in doubt until we lost the centre of our universe, my ma, my poor wee ma. But that's for later.

This is a tale of a family that fought to survive the tribulations of life in late-twentieth-century Glasgow: with joy, pain and delight and despair in various forms but always with a sense of humour intact. I hope you enjoy reading it as much as I enjoyed writing it, and even more so, living it. I hope it truly reflects the immense love I was blessed with as a child but didn't appreciate until I was much older. I hope it also reflects the deep and everlasting gratitude I have that I was born into the family I was born into, and a profound appreciation of my shared life with them.

By the way, before anybody goes 'radio rental' this isn't actually a completely true story. Most of the things that happen in the book are based on an approximation of the truth. Most of the characters are based on my family and friends. I have the same number of siblings – seven – in real life as Danny McCallister. To all intents and purposes I am Danny McCallister. And he is me. We have a similar outlook on life and a similar abundant love of family.

Some of my siblings, and more particularly their children, have taken to addressing each other by their characters' names. My sister Christine loves her character, Darlene, and may well change her name to Darlene at some point. Christine empathises with Darlene, especially regarding her spoonerisms, but she said to me that she wishes she had some of Darlene's bravery and tenacity. The thing is she did, and does, have those qualities. She's the only one who doesn't realise it.

The situations I place those characters in throughout this series of books are not quite true, but based on the truth with a little embellishment thrown in. Poetic licence if you like. I have my family's permission to tell our story.

My nephews and nieces, and in some cases great nephews and nieces, desperately want to know if I am telling the truth about their parents and grandparents. Sometimes I am, sometimes I am not. But if it gets them talking and reminiscing, that's all to the good. Isn't it?

My family gladly gave their permission because it is a positive story, a happy story, a story of ordinary Glaswegians, more widely of ordinary people. A life story that has good bits and bad bits; like all life stories. We aren't ashamed or worried or in any way embarrassed about the bad bits; they made us who we are, and we like who we are. Most of the time.

So if you are a friend of mine, a member of my extended family, or if you even just grew up near Cessnock during the Seventies and Eighties, let me answer your question before you e-mail, text, Skype or tweet me.

'No, it isnae you.'

There may be a facet of you or your caricature. But it isn't the real you. The real you is infinitely more interesting than anything I could make up.

Now please read it. Laugh, cry and enjoy it but, I repeat, I know it sounds like you and I know it's the type of thing you might have done, and I know you remember doing something just like it. But honest to goodness, it wisnae you.

I would tell you if it was.

Cliff McCabe,
Glasgow,
September 2015

1

It was going to be a great day. A day we had been eagerly anticipating.

'Where the hell is he then, Daniel? He was supposed to come home with you,' Maggie McCallister berated me, her nine-year-old son, for not looking after my seven-year-old brother, Charlie.

'I don't know where he is Ma. He came back with me from school and then disappeared. Am I supposed to tie him to my wrist?'

For a split second I thought my ma hadn't noticed my insolence. But my big sister, Dot, had and she clouted me across the back of the head while launching into her own tirade about how careless I had been in letting Charlie out of my sight. Ordinarily, there wouldn't have been a problem as the school was only two hundred yards from our tenement close. But today wasn't an ordinary day. Today was the day we had moved a mile-and-a-half away to a new tenement flat. And, would you believe, it had three bedrooms.

I was standing in the hallway of the new flat being shouted at from four different directions and five different people. But I could barely hear them such was my astonishment at the amount of space that surrounded me. We had come from a room-and-kitchen flat and that is an accurate description. It was literally one room with a kitchen off, with the kitchen having a recessed alcove to accommodate a double bed, or, in our case, two sets of bunk beds.

It was a tight squeeze at the best of times, but the strangest thing was that most of the time we didn't moan about it. In the 'room' part of the room and kitchen there were two double beds, one of which was behind a curtain that stretched diagonally across part of the room, from one side of the window to a point just inside the door.

The curtain was hung on what amounted to a clothes line. It gave my parents a little privacy, bearing in mind that behind the curtain there was also a cot in which Paul, my youngest brother at the time, slept. In the opposite corner of the room was the second double bed. This was where my sisters, Dorothy and Darlene, slept. I recall the occasional argument about space for clothes or the use of underwear, make-up and toiletries.

Perhaps surprisingly, the squabbles were not that frequent and not that heated. When I think of the way the two girls fought after we had moved to Cessnock, for the silliest of reasons, it comes as a shock that they co-existed in such a tight space. Maybe I was too young and uninterested to notice; maybe they fought all the time.

The recessed alcove area in the kitchen could accommodate a double bed and, if you were lucky, a sideboard. In our case there were two sets of bunk beds, along either side of the alcove, with about two-and-a-half feet between them. In the deepest part of the alcove we had two tallboys, one on top of the other.

These contained our clothes, with the exception of our outside jackets, which were hung on a row of hooks in the hall. Hall is a rather grand description of that space. It was three feet wide and eight feet long, and had three doors off, one leading to the 'room', one to the 'kitchen' and the third to a cupboard that my ma called the scullery. It also had a three-row pulley, as did both the room and the kitchen.

When it was too cold or wet to hang a washing in the back court, the three pulleys were utilised. If you were unlucky enough to come in just after my ma had hung the washing you had to dash to avoid the water dripping from the clothes. Although we had a wringer it was an old one and took a lot of effort to use. My ma, as always, did her best but could have used some help from my da. Fat chance of that.

The two sets of bunk beds were used by me, my two older brothers, Donnie and Duncan, and, of course, Charlie. My da had a rule that the bedwetters should sleep on the bottom. He reasoned that it was bad enough getting rained on from the pulleys, without being peed on from above as well. I have to admit I was on one of the bottom bunks, while Duncan was on the other.

Now in our new place I was looking at eight doors. Two were only cupboards, which held a huge linen closet and a coal bunker. Three doors opened up into bedrooms, one into a kitchen and one into a living room. But the last was incredible. It opened up to reveal a *bathroom*, a bathroom with a WC, basin and full-size bath. No more standing in a queue every morning to use the close toilet, or to empty the pos that we had used during the night.

We always prayed that today it would be somebody else's turn to open the door. We had good reason to be apprehensive. It wasn't unusual to find a rat sitting on the toilet seat cleaning its whiskers and looking at you as if you had no right to be disturbing its morning routine.

The stairhead toilets were by far the worst part of living in McLean Street. That was the same for any tenement with outside toilets. It wasn't just the chance of meeting a fat, hairy rat with delusions of grandeur. It was the smell, which was truly awful. I learned, as all the boys did, to pee quickly while holding my nose with one hand and my willy with the other. Having to sit down was torture. We trained our bowels. We did our number twos at school and used the stairhead toilet only when desperate.

Don't get me wrong. My ma did her best to keep it clean. She used enough bleach to float a battleship. But it was a losing battle. On our landing there were three houses, which meant that at least twenty-five people were using one toilet pan. It had a chain-pull cistern above it but, when you flushed, the amount of water released was pitiful. A floater was almost guaranteed every time you went. Dorothy told me that she would go into pubs and risk being thrown out, or propositioned, rather than use that toilet.

One thing I do remember clearly is that all of us, with the exception of my ma, spent as little time indoors as possible. I would never be in before dark, even when I was only seven or eight. I stayed out as long as possible. Dorothy constantly found excuses to be with friends as did Donnie. Duncan and Darlene were too young to stay out overnight, but, like me, they would spend the hours between teatime and bedtime on the street.

So here I was in our new house looking at a bathroom that we didn't have to share with anyone. It was for us and us alone. I had overheard my ma and da talking about this new house, and one of them saying it had a bathroom, but I didn't understand what they meant. I thought it was going to be a cupboard in which you could keep the battered tin bath we used every Sunday, even though some among us had to be plunged in and held down to be washed.

So they could shout at me about Charlie as much as they wanted. I was determined to take in every nook and cranny of my new home. That's what it was instantly: our new home, not our new house, but our new *home*. I could feel it, the unstoppable future rushing towards us. I was too young to know what the feeling was but it was there all the same. I knew this would be the backdrop to everything that was ever going to matter to us. All manner of things would start and end right here.

But first things first. Where had Charlie gone? This wasn't the first time he had dropped me in it. It most certainly wouldn't be the last.

At this point in our lives there were nine of us, headed by our parents, David and Maggie, The roll call of children, from the oldest to the youngest, was, Donald (20), Dorothy (18), Duncan (14), Darlene (13), me (Daniel, 9), Charlie (7) and Paul (six months). David junior would join us a year later. Apparently, the new baby made it necessary for us to move as the room and kitchen was sufficient for eight but not nine.

It wasn't even really my ma or my da who decided we should move. It was the 'green lady' who came to see us when Paul was born. Glasgow's green ladies were health visitors employed by the council, so-called because they wore green uniforms and long green coats. Our green lady was outraged at our living conditions and bullied the local councillor into taking action. It was him, according to my ma, who pulled the necessary strings. And then, lo and behold, we were allocated a council house.

It was a council property, owned by Glasgow Corporation, as was every other house in the street. My da would never have dreamt of trying to buy a house. For a start he was always in and out of work so no bank or building society would have touched him with a bargepole. My sister Dorothy told me that we were always running out of private factors because we would have to do moonlight flits every time my da had no money to pay the rent, which was a regular occurrence.

Of course, my ma did her best to make Da's wages last from one Friday to the next but that was easier said than done. He would either spend too much on drink or come home with short wages because he hadn't worked a full week. Then there was only one alternative: the pawn shop. We had little of value. Sometimes it was my da's funeral suit – so called because it was the only time he wore it – or my ma's engagement and wedding rings. Neither the suit nor the rings had much value, but the £2 or so we got would see Ma through the week.

People talk about a hand-to-mouth existence. We lived it.

You may be wondering why my parents dropped the theme of starting their children's names with a 'D' when it came to Charlie. It was because my da was working away from home when Charlie was born and my uncle Charlie was instrumental in getting my ma to hospital when she went into labour. After that they named the last two of my brothers Paul and David, honouring my maternal grandfather and my da respectively.

Duncan and Darlene were hurriedly dispatched to the old house. There was a chance that Charlie had slipped back to play with his friends. The fact that the house was over a mile-and-a-half away via a complicated route, a route that crossed a minimum of three busy roads, was deemed insufficient to deter Charlie. A jungle, desert or combat zone wouldn't deter Charlie from going where Charlie wanted to go. Duncan and Darlene were chosen to look for him because Donald and my da were at work, while Dot was needed to look after Paul and help with the unpacking.

'Unpacking' is stretching it.

The lion's share of our possessions was the ragtag furniture, which had been transported on a horse and cart earlier that morning while we had been at school. (The same horse and cart would play a significant role in my oldest brother's life just a couple of months later.) There was a three-piece suite that had been in pretty good nick fifteen years before, when it was bought second-hand. Now it had replacement legs, which my da had cut off an old sideboard, and sheets of plywood nailed underneath the cushions to prevent your arse falling through and hitting the floor. Then there was a long table that had obviously begun its life in a canteen, with its tubular metal legs and melamine top. There was a collection of about eight chairs, no more than two of which matched. And there were two double beds and two sets of bunk beds.

For storage there were two or three chests of drawers, of varying sizes, and an old sideboard with no legs. Then, finally, there was my ma's pride and joy: the ornamental glass display cabinet, filled with plaster of Paris ornaments picked up on school trips to Saltcoats and Ayr, although when I say picked up, I mean won at the fair. And that was that. Our total assets wouldn't have filled a garden shed.

It was already very dark. After all it was half-past five on a dreich, miserable, November afternoon in Glasgow.

'He will come back soon,' I said. 'His stomach will be thinking his throat has been cut.'

The look on my ma's face told me that using a phrase about throats being cut, when my seven-year-old brother had been missing for almost two hours, wasn't at all helpful. And the slap on the back of the head from Dot confirmed I wasn't nearly as funny as I thought I was.

But I wasn't worried about Charlie. I knew the little shit wouldn't be far away. He would probably be playing football or kick the can or jumping walls with new-found friends. I was more worried about the time. My da would be home in less than half an hour and if Charlie hadn't turned up by then I would be for the high jump. I could almost feel the leather belt across the back of my legs. There was only one thing for it, hide. I could have gone looking for the little shit but much easier to conceal myself somewhere warm with a book and wait for him to come home and get my ma's undivided attention, as per usual.

So where to find a suitable cranny? It had to be somewhere that I could use for a while because with the number of lunatics in this asylum a good bolthole was a necessity. There was a huge cupboard in the hallway; one that my ma had decided was an ideal place to put the old sideboard, in which she kept all her sheets and towels. The sideboard didn't take up the complete width of the cupboard; there was a gap on the right-hand side of about two feet. My plan was to climb onto the sideboard and squeeze into the narrow gap. I could hide until my little brother turned up and everybody calmed down.

My cunning plan failed because as soon as I dropped my feet into the space, there was a scream. 'Daniel, you're standing on my head, you shitebag.'

The voice belonged to one Charles McCallister.

At the sound of his voice Dot and my ma came running in. Of course, it was me who was in hot water. While my ma shouted, Dot yet again clipped me on the side of the head. So there I was, having extricated myself from Charlie's head, watching him being cuddled by Ma and having his hair tousled by Dot.

'Are you okay Charlie? Come and get something to eat son. You must be starving,' Ma said.

How does that work, I thought? The little shit goes missing, deliberately as far as I could tell, and when he turns up, he gets fed and cuddled and I get slapped.

It would be a recurring theme. Charlie screwed up, Daniel was punished.

2

The first month in our new home, leading up to Christmas 1970, was magical. For the first week we were waiting for new furniture and appliances, including a cooker from Fisher's, a credit warehouse in the centre of Glasgow. It meant that for a week we survived on sandwiches, mostly cheese or salmon paste.

On Thursday nights, my da's payday, we got a chippy. Ambrosia, the food of the gods, is the only way to describe it. We were allowed a sausage supper or a pie supper because they were the cheapest. My da got a fish supper, while my ma got a 'special' fish supper. This was the crème de la crème of luxury food in Kinning Park at the time – a slab of whiting done in breadcrumbs instead of batter.

More exciting fare was on its way. A new Chinese takeaway had opened recently and some Indian guys had been looking at a shop on Paisley Road West and the people next door said it might become a restaurant too. All manner of exotic wonders were blossoming on our doorstep, but that was all a bit fancy for us. We were delighted to stick to a chippy, thank you very much.

When the furniture and appliances eventually arrived, two weeks before Christmas, we felt like royalty. The whole street came to have a gander when the big lorry trundled up to our close and the guys in brown warehouse coats began carrying an impressive array of white goods up the stairs. There was a brand-new electric cooker, a fridge and a twin-tub washing machine.

I heard one neighbour tell another, 'That's the latest model you know. Look at it. It's beautiful. I wonder why these McCallisters have moved in here. If they can afford all this they should be living in Kelvinside.'

The second neighbour chuckled. 'They can't afford it, you halfwit. Look at the lorry. It's from Fisher's, on tick. Mark my words. Right after the New Year that lorry will be back repossessing the whole lot.'

They walked away chuckling and missed the unloading of the new telly. They also missed my ma's dream come true: a new three-piece suite. It would be three months before the plastic wrapping came off the suite and anybody got to plant their arse on it.

It was during the unloading that I met my new friends: Searcher and Bobby the Bear. They were about my age and while Searcher was a bit shorter than me Bobby the Bear was at least five-and-a-half-feet tall, which, for a nine-year-old in Glasgow, made him a freak. He weighed in at eight stone, hence Bobby the Bear.

Searcher got his nickname because of his unparalleled skill in raking through middens. He was so good that his da would take him and his brother all over the south-side of Glasgow to search middens for luckies. This was almost a nightly occurrence, straight after the boys got out of school. You would see them coming back at eight o'clock, their handcart piled high with clothing and junk.

It was certainly junk. But Searcher's da was brilliant at fixing it up and selling it from his stall at the Barras on Saturday and Sunday mornings. He must have been good because it provided the entire income on which all fourteen of the O'Donnells survived.

It was Searcher who made the first move as Charlie and I stood proudly watching our new possessions being delivered.

'Hoy, wee man,' he shouted at me.

It didn't matter to Searcher that I was two inches taller, one of the very few people over whom I had a height advantage. To him, everybody was 'hoy wee man'. I looked round and saw this skinny little boy wearing filthy trousers and a woollen pullover that must have belonged to his big sister, being pink and three sizes too big.

'What?' I responded, a bit warily, particularly when I spotted the giant beside him with the vacant facial expression.

Charlie wasn't so reticent. 'All right Searcher. What are you up to?

How are you no' out midgie-raking with Anthony and Cleopatra?' he asked, referring to Searcher's twin siblings.

'It's Anthony and Caroline, no' Cleopatra ya daftie.' This broke the ice admirably and Bobby the Bear broke in.

'Hurry up Searcher. Before it's too late,' he said, shiftily.

'Before what's too late?' I asked, wary again, noticing Bobby looking around, swaying nervously from foot to foot.

'It's all right wee man, don't shit your pants. Keep a look out for the delivery men coming back down your stairs. They've left their jackets in the front of the lorry. That means they don't care about them. They now belong to us, ta very much,' Searcher concluded.

Although his logic seemed to be a bit off, I said to Charlie, 'Go and stand at the close and when you hear the men coming down the stairs, start shouting and bawling that you've hurt your leg or something.'

As Charlie nonchalantly sauntered over to the close, obviously delighted that we had been invited into this criminal enterprise, I began to have second thoughts. If anybody saw what we were doing I would be spending Christmas putting Germoline on the belt marks my da would leave across the backs of my legs and on my arse. I turned round, fully intending to tell this wee boy I would later call my best friend, 'No way pal. Keep us out of it.'

I was a fraction of a second too late. Bobby was leaping out of the open door of the lorry with a bundle under each arm while Searcher had taken off like greased lightning, heading for his own close, which was directly across the street from mine.

Unfortunately, Bobby didn't do grease lightning. Bobby did lumbering and tripping over his own feet and crashing head first into the wall of Searcher's close. Luckily, Searcher grabbed him and dragged him up the close before anybody spotted them. The delivery men were still too busy at the back of the lorry to be bothered about what two eejits were doing across the street.

Within thirty seconds Searcher's head appeared, hanging out of his bedroom window on the third floor. He shouted across, 'Danny, Charlie. Are youse coming up here to play?'

I walked towards his close but was forced to turn back when I heard Charlie screaming.

'Somebody help me. I've broke my leg. Please mammy, daddy, mammy, daddy. Somebody help me. It's hinging aff. Oh please, please, help me.'

By the time I reached him the delivery men were beside him: 'What's up son? What have you done?'

And so were half the neighbours. Charlie looked at me and winked. When I shook my head and glanced over my shoulder to indicate that the deed was done, and there was no need for his charade, Charlie leapt to his feet and cried, 'It's okay. It's no' broke. I thought it was broke. I fell and heard something snapping. But I think it might have been the bar of toffee in my pocket. No harm done. Go about your business. There's nothing more to see.'

I grabbed him by the hair and dragged him away before his rank stupidity got us caught. When we got to Searcher's he had the three jackets laid out on his bed. But before I even glanced at them I was looking around his room with wonder and delight.

'That's a great idea,' I said. 'I'm going to ask my da if he would do this to our room.'

Searcher realised what I was talking about and burst out laughing. 'Ya tube. My da didny wallpaper the walls with old papers and comics to give us a laugh. It's all we had. He widny spend good money on wallpaper. Are you radio rental?'

'But there's wallpaper on the hall and living-room walls. I seen it as I was coming in,' I replied.

He again responded with a laugh.

'Go and look again, ya eejit. There's about ten different types of paper on each wall. Whenever we go midgie-raking and I find bits of wallpaper that people had left over from doing their house up, I bring it hame and my da sticks it on the walls. The more paper you can put on the longer it takes the mould to get through.'

As he said this I noticed the black mould around the corners of the windows and where the wall met the ceiling. Searcher's room had four sets of bunk beds. The one against the furthest wall had a curtain in front, hanging on a wire suspended from the ceiling.

Searcher saw me looking. 'That's where my big sisters sleep. The curtains are so that we canny see their tits or anything when they're going to bed.'

Before that image had a chance to form in my mind I noticed Bobby looking through the pockets of the stolen jackets. 'There's bugger all in these jaikets. Not a single penny. The miserable bastards have got nothing.'

Searcher said, 'Gimme a look.' He caressed every square inch of the first jacket, paying particular attention to the areas around the pockets. He delved into the left pocket and after rummaging around for a few seconds his hand emerged with a roll of money. His face lit up with a grin.

'I knew it. When we find a man's jacket in the bins, my old man always tells me to check the lining near the pockets. A lot of the old guys slip a few quid in there to hide it from their wives, because they go through their pockets when they're drunk.'

He unrolled the little bundle and discovered it amounted to five single pound notes.

'One for you, one for you, one for you and two for me,' he said gleefully, as he divided the spoils four ways.

A pound note in 1970 didn't make you rich beyond your wildest dreams. But it would pay for a night at the pictures or a right big bag of sweeties.

'What should we do Searcher? Do you think we should go to the Lyceum this afternoon and see what pictures are showing? Or will we go along to George's cafe and get a burger and an iced drink?' Bobby asked, while staring in wonderment at the pound note stretched between his hands.

Searcher laughed. 'Youse three can do what youse want, but my two quid is getting tucked away with the rest of my dosh. I like to put it aside for a rainy day. Bobby, for god's sake. Stop staring at it, will you. It's only a pound.'

'I've never had a pound to myself wee man. It's all right for you putting money away for a rainy day. I've never had any money and it's always fuckin' raining for me,' Bobby sighed, trying to explain his captivation with the grubby pound note he continued to stare at.

I was still wary of these two characters. They knew my name and were friendly enough. But I had known them five minutes and was already an opportunist thief. If there was one thing my father detested it was someone who stole from his own.

'Here,' I said, taking the pound from Charlie's hand, adding my pound and handing them to Bobby. 'Youse two can have it all. We never really done anything anyway.'

Bobby put his hand out to take the cash but Searcher slapped it away.

'Wait a minute ya big eejit. What do you mean you never done anything? Daniel, you wouldn't be thinking of grassing us up. Would you pal?'

Before I could defend my position, and explain my da's abhorrence of thievery, Charlie grabbed the two quid. 'I did do something for this money. I put on a good performance. I'm keeping my pound and if he doesn't want his then I'm claiming it since I'm his wee brother.'

Searcher smiled. 'Well done wee man. Your head is screwed on properly, unlike your big brother's.'

I was in a pickle. Charlie now had two quid and by taking the moral high ground I had done myself out of a pound. But then again I was nine, nearly ten, and still allowed to change my mind without an inquisition. I took hold of Charlie by the ear and grabbed my pound back.

'Okay then, I'll take it. But if my da finds out we're dead,' I said to Charlie. The smile on his face at getting to keep his pound highlighted the difference between us, which would become ever more apparent as we got older.

I worried, he enjoyed.

3

As Charlie and I wandered across the street to our house he glanced at me slyly. 'We could probably use this money to get my ma a present for her Christmas. But then my da might want to know where we got so much money and we would be in trouble. So maybe we better spend it on sweeties after all, eh?'

He finished what he had to say in a rush because, as we were about to enter the close, Darlene came skipping out, took Charlie by the hands and danced the Dashing White Sergeant with him. 'I've got my own room. I've got my own room, away from the smelly wee bastards,' she sang over and over.

I laughed at Charlie, who had started to sing along with her. 'Hey stupid arse. You're the smelly wee bastard she's singing about.'

'I know. I'm just really happy for her. Because she's got the ghost in her room,' he said innocently, continuing to dance in a circle with Darlene.

Darlene stopped swinging him so abruptly, with the result that Charlie stumbled and fell into the hedge that belonged to the garden of the house on the ground floor. I say garden. It measured about ten feet by two feet, and because the hedge was about four foot tall, Charlie almost disappeared into it.

'What's he talking about Daniel? What does he mean the room with the ghost in it? The wee shite's lying. Isn't he? Isn't he, Daniel?' Darlene squealed, panic-stricken.

As usual Charlie had been able to squash Darlene's happiness in the blink of an eye. Darlene had a sunny disposition. Every morning when she woke up she burst into life, instinctively optimistic about the day ahead. Sometimes that enthusiasm could last all day, unless that is Charlie got to her first.

I almost always took Darlene's side in any dispute with Charlie. In fact I almost always took anybody's side in a dispute with Charlie. I worked on the premise that he was a lying wee shite until proven beyond reasonable doubt that he wasn't. To be fair I was correct in my assumption most of the time. But on this occasion I decided, on the spur of the moment, that it was too good an opportunity to miss.

'I think he might be telling the truth, Darlene. We were up at Searcher's house and his granny was telling us that the reason we got this house was because the last family that lived there did a runner in the middle of the night. Their granny died in the front bedroom and was coming back every night, not believing that she was really dead. Not just that. She had a habit of climbing into the bed of whoever was in that room. They got a priest to bless it but not even that worked.'

The tearful look on Darlene's face made me feel terrible. I was about to relent and tell her it was a joke, when I glanced at Charlie's face. The mixture of awe and glee on his coupon won me over to the dark side.

'Maybe the old dear wants to live again in the body of a wee lassie,' I suggested, with my most serious look.

'Ma,' Darlene screamed as she swept back into the close and raced up the stairs three at a time. 'Ma, gonny tell them two. They're trying to scare me,' she blurted out as she reached the second floor and our front door.

Within thirty seconds the window of our front room was thrown open. My ma's head emerged and she uttered one word: 'in'.

I looked at Charlie and he looked at me and we both glanced up to make sure that my ma had backed away from the window. We burst out laughing, and, as we entered the close still in fits, I grabbed Charlie by the arm. 'By the way, you're right wee man.'

I grabbed him round the neck with one arm, trapped one of his legs between mine and plunged my other hand into the pocket of his trousers. It emerged with the pound note that Searcher had given him. I told him, 'We will be using this to buy my ma and my da something for Christmas.'

I sprinted up the stairs before he had time to object. But as I looked back over my shoulder sniggering, and saw his black look, I wondered when I would be paying for this. Because I *would* be paying, one way or another.

As I fell through our front door into the hallway, Charlie was right behind me, punching my back and screaming, 'You can't do that. You can't do that. It's not fair.'

My ma emerged from the kitchen, wiping her hands on the apron that was tied round her waist. 'What is it now? Can you two not just get on for one bloody day?' she asked, as she swiped at me with a dish towel. She wrestled Charlie away from me and said, 'He can't do what? What has he done to you?'

This gave the little shit an opening. 'Aw Ma, he told me there's a ghost in this house and it will probably be coming after me or Darlene tonight.' Charlie managed to cry through every word of this lie but, strangely, when my ma turned round and slapped me on the back of the head the tears were replaced by a huge grin.

'That's it, Daniel. Enough is enough,' each word accompanied by a slap. She had a hold of my jacket with one hand and was slapping at the back of my head with the other. I had my hands on my head, trying to get some protection from her swipes.

'I didn't tell him that Ma. It was him that was trying to frighten Darlene. It wasn't me. Ask Darlene.'

As I pleaded with my ma, Darlene walked into the hallway from the kitchen. When my ma looked at her for confirmation of what I was saying, Darlene put the same bloody grin on her face that Charlie had on his. 'Daniel was trying to frighten both of us Ma. He was out of order.'

My ma dragged me along the hall by the hood of my jacket, causing the pullover and shirt I had on underneath to ride up my back until they almost came off over my head. My bare back was exposed, presenting a handy target for my ma to deliver a stinging slap. 'Get in that bloody room and stay there. No tea for you and just wait till your da comes in. You're going to know all about it boy.'

I sat on the bottom bunk, dazed, and pulled my clothes down to cover my exposed midriff. Sobbing, I wondered how it had happened.

Charlie made up a story to frighten Darlene; I joined in for a laugh. Darlene and Charlie were now sitting in the warm kitchen wiring into tea and toast with jam. Here I was in a freezing bedroom with a slapped head, waiting for my da to come in and add his hand prints to my ma's.

How the hell did that happen?

As usual the fear of what my da might do to me was much greater than the reality. He came in, listened to the case for the prosecution, which was led by my ma with screeched evidence from Darlene and Charlie. He solemnly passed judgement. I was guilty as charged and would spend the weekend in my room.

I railed against this miscarriage of justice. 'That's not fair. Charlie started all this and him and Darlene were ganging up to get me into bother, like they always do.'

My da listened patiently. Then he advised me that as an alternative to the first punishment, I could spend the weekend in my room but have a sore arse as well, if that's what I really wanted.

I almost blurted out, 'That doesn't make any sense. Why would I want a sore arse as well?' But I realised that he was being facetious and the wisest thing to do was shut up and accept that I was under house arrest for the weekend.

I tried to turn away in a huff and storm into my bedroom. But the defiant exit I had intended never happened. I tripped over Charlie's discarded jacket and crashed head first into the wall beside my bedroom door. It heightened the comedic effect for everyone else, but brought me no comfort.

I sobbed my way along the hall and threw myself on to the bottom bunk as the sounds of their laughter hurried me along.

4

The rest of that week and the weekend I spent in my room passed peacefully enough, except for the pigeon incident. My brother Duncan was four years older than me but the gap in maturity between a ten-year-old and a fourteen-year-old is immense. In my eyes he was almost a man. He had a girlfriend, a full-time job – having recently left school – and, unbelievably, a gun.

Well, I say a gun. It was an air rifle, a very old air rifle. Although it fired lead pellets or tiny darts, it did so with the gusto of a ninety-nine-year-old man blowing out the candles on his birthday cake. But for a boy sent to his room for a crime he didn't commit it was a godsend. That, at least, was my initial reaction.

My acquisition of Dunky's gun happened on the Sunday afternoon. I had finished every single piece of reading material in my room, my sisters' room, the living room, the kitchen and even the bathroom. I was bored rigid. In fact, bored isn't even close to being a strong enough word. It took an age for a second to pass. It got even worse when I looked out of my bedroom window and saw Charlie, Searcher and Bobby playing head tennis over the fence that separated our back court from the one opposite.

I decided to approach my ma again, for, oh, the twenty-ninth time that day and beg to be allowed out. Even if I had been guilty of the heinous crime of frightening my siblings with ghost stories – which I wasn't – the punishment handed down was barbaric.

And anyway, I had spent all day Saturday and the majority of Sunday in my bedroom and therefore I should be allowed the afternoon off for good behaviour. Then I considered what she had said when I had made my twenty-eighth appeal for clemency, just ten minutes earlier.

'Daniel, your da's still sleeping, probably still drunk from last night. Your brothers and sisters are all out. The house is lovely and quiet and I am sitting here with a cup of tea and a fag, watching *The Waltons*. If you don't get into your room and out of my sight within the next ten seconds I will wake your da up and you can whinge to him about how unfair he has been.'

This was delivered without her even bothering to turn away from the television.

I quietly huffed my way back into the bedroom shared by my brothers. I intended to search under Duncan's bed, to see if he had anything to read, not thinking for a minute that anything I found might be inappropriate for a ten-year-old.

There was no reading material. However, I did find Duncan's air rifle and a small, round, tin box full of lead pellets. I pondered whether this was a good idea or whether there was potential for more misery. It took me all of two seconds to make up my mind. I told myself not to be so dense. What possible problems could be caused with a stupid old air rifle that hardly worked?

I mused, who or what should I shoot at first? I tracked the rifle from left to right and then from right to left along the window sill.

'Charlie, Searcher,' I shouted. 'Go and get some tin cans from the midden and put them along the fence.' I waved the rifle from side to side as I shouted; a visual explanation of my request.

They hesitated. It is not in a Glaswegian boy's nature to do as he is told, without first examining the order and deciding whether he can derive any benefit from it or if it will cause him grief.

'How much?' Charlie shouted back, confused.

'Do you mean how many?' I answered my own question. 'About twenty.'

'No,' Charlie responded. 'I mean how much will you give me if I do it? Will you give me two bob?'

I was raging. Here I was stuck in the house for the whole weekend because of him. I had at last found something that might help me while away the time and the little shite was playing stupid bastards.

'It's not two bob Charlie. It's ten pence now,' was Bobby's contribution.

'Aye, so it is Charlie. But good shout wee man. It's got to be worth at least ten pence to go into the midden, find twenty cans and put them along the fence. Aye, good shout wee man,' Searcher added, smiling at Charlie, his new protégé.

All three of them craned their necks and looked up. They were waiting either for my decision or for the next gambit in the negotiation.

'If you don't do it by the time I count to five you wee shite, I am going to put a bullet right up your arsehole,' was my quite reasonable response.

Charlie laughed. 'You couldn't shoot me with that thing if I was standing on the window sill in front of you, ya tube.'

Searcher laughed. 'He's got a point Danny and, even if you could, do you think your ma will see that as a good thing or a bad thing? Shooting a lead pellet into your wee brother's arsehole, I mean?'

Bobby smiled and looked at Searcher adoringly, obviously inspired by his pal's wisdom. Once again Charlie had me in a corner. I couldn't shoot him. I don't mean I didn't want to or that the gun might not work properly. I did and it would. But Searcher was right. It wasn't the way to get back in either my ma or da's good books. But, equally, I didn't want to give the little shite ten pence and lose face in front of my recently acquired friends. It was a problem.

How could I get him to do it for nothing and so save face?

'After I knock them over you can all come up and have a go Charlie.' He immediately accepted this as an equitable solution. The three of them then spent twenty minutes selecting the correct combination of bottles, jars and tin cans. That little lot would constitute a test of my shooting skills equal to those faced by circus performers, cowboys or Olympic competitors.

They stood behind a low wall at least twenty feet away from the array of bottles and cans before I began shooting. It showed a complete lack of confidence in my ability. I managed to prove them at least partially correct when my first shot missed its intended target by inches and ricocheted off a fence. When the rogue pellet struck the wall that the three amigos were standing behind they questioned both my intelligence and my parentage.

'What are you doing you stupid bastard? That nearly pierced my ear,' was Searcher's succinctly put query.

'Well don't stand so close, you bunch of eejits.'

Bobby looked up, a venomous look on his face. 'We're not standing too close. You're just a fanny at shooting.'

'Fair point,' I conceded, and laughed again.

The next ten minutes were again spent in negotiations. The result was that I would be allowed seventeen shots. That was the total number of targets on display. So I could have a crack at them all. The other three would then have the same opportunity and whoever hit the most targets would be the winner.

We spent another ten minutes ironing out a comprehensive scoring system, one that only young boys could conceive. The gist of it was that a smashed bottle or jar was worth ten points and any lesser damage would be decided on a sliding scale of one to ten.

It was a very enjoyable afternoon and we got through a high percentage of Duncan's tin, which probably held a thousand pellets. I made a mental note to blame Charlie if Duncan ever noticed.

Searcher was winning with a total of 314 points. This would have been more had Charlie and I not robustly disputed his award to himself of ten points for a tin can being pierced. His reasoning was that this was equivalent to a jar being smashed because the tin can could no longer hold liquids.

We countered by pointing out that the can had contained boiled ham and was therefore still fit for purpose. Searcher tried to settle the argument by threatening to go home if we didn't stop cheating. Although it was a moving argument, Charlie's response of, 'Don't let the close door hit you on the arse on the way out,' won the day.

I was lining up the sights on the first target of my final round of shots when Bobby said, 'Look Danny'. He was pointing at a pigeon that had landed on a pipe. The pipe ran horizontally below my window, about thirty feet down. The cushy doo settled into position and seemed ready to spend the afternoon there. Perhaps it was watching us enjoying ourselves or, more likely, waiting for us to go so that it could look for worms or a scrap of bread.

I was about to resume my target practice when Searcher cupped his hands together in front of his mouth and stage whispered, 'shoot it'. I hesitated only briefly before leaning out across the sill, aiming and firing.

As I pulled the trigger I heard Charlie ask, 'Why?'

And before the pellet hit its intended target, which could only have taken a hundredth of a second, I asked myself the same question.

The pellet struck the pigeon on the breast, knocking it from the pipe to the ground. The wounded bird writhed around silently, its tiny brain trying in vain to work out a reason for its distress and its inability to either walk or fly.

After a few seconds it gave up the mental and physical struggle and died.

Charlie looked up at me, bewildered. It was a look that broke my ten-year-old heart, a look that represented the fall of his hero. I didn't know it then, but I know it now. To that point he had unquestioning faith in me and his tender young mind couldn't find an excuse for what I had done.

Neither could I. I cried inside and out. Not because what I had done was wrong, although I instinctively knew that, but because I could see the anguish I had caused my brother.

I was crying for Charlie.

Searcher was stunned, as was Bobby, when I shouted, 'You told me to do it. That was your fault.'

I thought of what my da said whenever I tried to blame someone else for telling me what to do. 'If he told you to jump in the Clyde, would you do it?'

Of course I wouldn't.

So why did I pull the trigger. Even now, forty years later, I am not sure. Was it bravado? Was it a momentary lapse, with no regard for the consequences? I honestly don't know, but the vision of that innocent little pigeon silently writhing, dying in our back court, haunts me still.

I don't know why, but it does.

5

My punishment was over. It was only four days before Christmas and the excitement was building. The chances were that this would be a very good Christmas indeed. My da and my oldest brother, Donald, had been working for most of the year. Although they were scaffolders to trade they had managed to secure labouring jobs on the construction of the M8 motorway, which would pass less than a quarter of a mile from our house.

This was the only time I could remember my da being continuously in work for such a long period. Normally he was employed from February till November and was laid off over the winter. So it was the considered opinion of both Charlie and I that this could be a bumper Christmas. The problem was that when we pestered our da about what Santa was going to bring we got his standard response: 'When I was a wean, all I ever got was an orange – and a doo-dit-doo-doo.'

We had learned not to ask what a doo-dit-doo-doo was. When he caught the unwary visitor with this long-running joke and they asked for an explanation, he would hold the cardboard tube from a toilet roll up to his mouth and blow, 'doo dit doo doo'. He was mimicking the rallying call of a trumpet.

The preparations for Christmas were always intense. The house had to be cleaned from top to bottom, or, if money permitted, redecorated. But as this was our first Christmas in the new place, and it had been decorated by the council before we moved in, my ma grudgingly accepted it would only be cleaned this time around. She was keen for the living room, at least, to have new wallpaper. But that was vetoed by my da, who thought 99 per cent of Christmas was nonsense.

And clean it we did. We set about the task with vigour because we knew the quicker it was cleaned the sooner we could hang the decorations and see presents appear below the tree. When we had finished, the whole place was sparkling. When my da got back from work he said we could rent the kitchen floor to the Southern General as an operating theatre, it was that clean.

Time to hang the decorations. My da, under pressure from my ma and the rest of us, had brought home a brand-new, green-plastic tree about three-foot high, a handful of tinsel and a dozen Christmas baubles. We had thrown out the old ones before moving. They had seen better days. In fact the better days they had seen were probably before I was born.

There was no real tree for us. That was for the posh people up in Pollokshields or Kings Park. But we were ecstatic with the shiny plastic one, if a little underwhelmed with the amount of decorations my da brought home. 'This is a big house David. That wee drop of tinsel won't get noticed in here,' my ma said when he brought them in.

Da flashed her a look that we were all familiar with: 'be grateful and shut up,' it said. We held our breath, hoping she would heed the warning.

'But it doesn't matter. The weans will make plenty more, won't you?' she replied, looking at us for support. For a split second no one uttered a word. Then Charlie, as usual, broke the silence.

'I want to make paper chains. I'm not making them knitted bauble things. They're rubbish,' he exclaimed.

Then we all joined in.

'I'll help with the paper chains Ma. And I'll do some knitted baubles as well if you want,' I chipped in.

Duncan repeated everything I said, but with a sarcastic undertone in a mocking, squeaky voice. He pushed me onto the floor but before I could get up and start hitting back, Charlie was on him with a flurry of punches to his ribs.

'Get off me, you wee shite,' Duncan cried, pushing Charlie away and slapping him at the same time.

Before I could wade in again my ma whacked Duncan across the back of his head, 'Enough, the three of you. Pack it in. I mean it. Just pack it in.'

Duncan's face told its own story: he had won again. Charlie's said different. In his mind it was normal, and perfectly okay, for him to hit me. But if anybody else, other than my parents, lifted a hand to me he was at them like a terrier. He was my personal bodyguard and whatever would happen between us he always would be.

Darlene then starting slapping Duncan, 'You spoil everything,' she was wailing.

Now it was my ma's turn to scream.

'For god's sake stop it. It's like a bloody mad house in here. Duncan, go away, right now, go away. Darlene, go and fetch that box of sticky paper and my old balls of wool out of the kitchen cupboard. Daniel, Charles, you two into the living room and sit on your arses for a minute. In fact, one of you get a hold of Paul and settle him down.'

Paul was in the living room strapped into his Silver Cross pram. I think that pram was originally mine or Charlie's. It had been used for the last four or five years to take my ma's washing to the steamie at Kinning Park baths. But after a good wash, and having had the dents on the side straightened out by my da, it was as good as new.

Paul was sitting up in the pram and screaming at the top of his lungs, presumably to fit in with everyone else. Charlie approached and started rubbing the top of his head gently. At the same time he leant down and said, 'What's up wee man? Never mind that lot. Charlie's here now.'

Paul quietened down, but not before a sharp intake of breath and a hitching sob produced a snot bubble that covered his face, 'Aah, you horrible wee monster,' Charlie laughed, as he leapt back from the eruption of snotters. Paul found this funny and began to chuckle, which caused his snot bubble to pulsate. It expanded to twice the original size, audibly popping and spreading all over his nose and chin. This caused the three of us to giggle uncontrollably for the next few minutes.

Darlene chose that precise moment to bounce into the living room and she immediately screeched, 'Ma, gonny tell them two. They're laughing at me now.'

'It's no wonder my hair is going grey. I'm surprised it's not falling out like your da's,' my ma sighed as we sat round the table, eager to start on the decorations.

'Right Charlie. You wanted to start the paper chains so you can do that. Darlene and Daniel will take care of the woollen baubles. Can you two remember what to do?' she asked, peering over her glasses.

Charlie was sitting with a pile of coloured tissue paper and sheets of coloured sticky paper. These were cut into strips, licked and then stuck together into a ring shape, interlocking them with the next piece to form a chain. The paper had come from my school, where both my ma and my sister, Dorothy, were cleaners.

Apparently, when they brought things home that didn't belong to them, it wasn't stealing. Oh no. It was a supplementary payment because they were on slave wages. So anything that could be secreted into a pocket or bag, or between layers of clothing, was fair game. Although this was contrary to my da's stated dislike of thieving, it was different. Because thieving from your employer was different. It wasn't thieving. It was making your wage up to a fair level. Everybody knew what went on. Even the bosses turned a blind eye.

The woollen baubles were made by cutting out a piece of cardboard shaped like a doughnut. Wool was then threaded round the ring until you had a tight ball, with another piece of wool used to attach the home-made bauble to the tree. I made one that fell apart at the seams and promptly decided that Darlene was much better at it than me. I would be more useful making the tea. Charlie made a paper chain that somehow incorporated one of his socks and several lengths of wool. Darlene decided for him that he didn't have the patience for paper chains. She transmitted this information by jabbing his bum with a darning needle. 'Why don't you piss off Charlie? All you're doing is making a mess.'

Charlie yelped, turned to my ma and asked: 'Gonny tell her ma? I'm not leaving a mess am I?' He said this with a straight face as my ma looked him up and down and saw the sticky paper that was stuck to his hair, collar, elbow and both knees. It was testament to his disregard for reality.

'No, Charlie. You're not leaving a mess son. You're taking it with you wherever you go,' she said, with a mother's indulgent smile.

* * *

'It's Christmas Eve, Danny. It's Christmas Eve, Danny. Get up.' Why Charlie had to punctuate this statement with head butts to my back as I lay asleep on my bottom bunk, I have no idea.

'For God's sake Charlie, that's sore. What's the matter with you? I know what day it is,' I grunted, throwing back the heavy blanket and sitting on the edge of the bed.

I looked at the little alarm clock I kept under the bed. It was seven o'clock and we didn't need to get up for school for another hour.

'Get up, get up, get up,' Charlie repeated, this time jumping behind me on the bed, applying a kick to my back every time he uttered the word 'up'.

'Right, that's it. I'm telling you. That's it,' I said, twisting round and grabbing for him as he scooted away laughing.

'Oh shit, it's freezing Charlie,' I whimpered as I pulled the blanket around me, shivering.

'You need to get up Danny. We have to wrap Ma and Da's presents and put them under the tree. Come on. Come on. Get up,' he insisted, trying to pull the blanket back off me.

As the tug of war over the blanket went on I heard the front door shutting and I said, 'Shut up you. There's my ma and Dot home from the school. Just shut up. We can wrap them later. But shut up before they come in.'

The truth is I was just as excited as he was. 'Charlie, when we finish at one, that's us off school until next year.'

'What are you talking about? We're off school for a year. How can we be?' he asked, perplexed.

'Because we don't start back until the fourth of January and that's next year. It's also next week and next month, but it's still next year,' I laughed, jumping out of bed and throwing the heavy blanket over Charlie.

By the time he had extricated himself, I was in the kitchen, sitting between my ma and Dot, out of his reach.

'Can we open one present this morning Ma? Before we go to school? Can we, can we?' Charlie pleaded, on entering the kitchen.

'How can you do that you eejit, when Santa hasn't even been yet?' Dot responded, laughing indulgently.

This left Charlie with a dilemma. We had already decided between us that Santa didn't exist and that, in fact, the presents were left by our parents. But, the problem was if we confessed to knowing that Santa didn't exist, it would take some of the shine off Christmas for them. It might also diminish our haul of presents. Better not to take the chance and continue to participate in the big lie that was Santa Claus.

'I mean one of the wee presents my granny left for me,' Charlie said, neatly extricating himself.

'No!' was my ma's response.

'Well what about we open one when we come in from school?' I suggested.

'No!'

'Well then, can we open one just before we go to bed?' was Charlie's final attempt.

My ma's response was to lower her newspaper and stare with *that* look. We knew the subject was closed and that further debate would not be in our best interests. It would also result in pain, Christmas Eve or no Christmas Eve. As I slipped out of the reach of both Ma and Dot, I said, 'Does that mean you'll think about it then?' and leapt out of the kitchen door laughing before a plate was thrown.

School that morning lasted forever. There is no way there was only four hours between nine in the morning and one in the afternoon. A fast runner could have gone to the moon and back in that time.

'Danny, Danny.' I was just about out of the gate when I heard my name being screamed by Charlie. His voice was coming from behind the toilet block in the school playground.

One boy, taller than me, had Charlie pinned in a corner, punching any part of his body that Charlie had left exposed. Another boy was watching. I leapt on the back of the puncher, trying to pull hair that wasn't there. He had, like most of us, a crew-cut. It meant less chance of nits.

I managed to get both arms around his neck and pull him away from Charlie. We fell in a heap, but luckily I remained on top. I was trying desperately to keep punching this boy before he got a chance to get up. He was huge and would probably beat my brains out if I let him get up.

Meanwhile I could hear Charlie shouting at my opponent. 'I told you Danny would batter you. I knew it. I told you.' Turning to the boy who was watching, he went on, 'I told you Danny would do him. You owe me two bob, you fanny.'

The boy underneath me was crying out 'keys, keys'. In schoolboy language it indicated he had had enough and was giving in. I had one hand on his neck while the other was raised to punch him. I told him: 'You said "keys". So if I let you go, you better not try to fight again.'

There were red marks all over his face and blood was dripping from the corner of his mouth. He turned his head and spat the blood out. Still crying he said, 'I didn't want to fight you. That wee bastard started on me for nothing.'

I banged his head against the ground. 'That wee bastard is my brother. If you call him a wee bastard again I will kick your balls right up into your throat and give you two sets of tonsils. Arsehole.'

I got up and grabbed Charlie by the collar. 'Right you wee bastard, move it,' I said, pulling him towards the school gate. I wanted to get away before the boy on the ground gathered his senses and came after us. He perhaps didn't realise, although I did, that without the element of surprise he would have wiped the floor with me.

So the wisest thing was to leave the scene, pronto. But Charlie didn't do wise. Even though I had a firm grip on the collar of his jersey he still managed to squirm round and hurl abuse at his tormentors: 'Jonto, I told you. You're a fanny. Willie, you owe me two bob. I better get it or you're next, you bastard.'

'Will you shut the fuck up Charlie? When we go back to school that Jonto will kill me. Look at the size of him and he's in primary seven as well. Why was he hitting you?' I asked, knowing I wouldn't like the answer.

Charlie slipped from my grasp, and straightened out his jersey, which had twisted until the front v-neck was between his shoulder blades. There was a broad grin on his face: 'I was having a wee bet with Willie that, to me, Jonto is a big fanny and in a fight you would batter him with one hand tied behind your back. For some reason, Jonto took offence and started punching me, big fanny that he is. He was lucky but if you hadn't turned up I was just about to kick his head in myself.'

I was in despair. I could have hit him. I could have shouted and screamed at him. But what would have been the point? It was Charlie. He had his own logic and I for one was not privy to the workings of that logic. I was merely a victim of it.

Admitting defeat, I put an arm affectionately around the back of his neck: 'Come on you wee shite. Let's get home before Jonto realises how wee I am and comes after us. Anyway, we need to wrap up the presents for my ma and da. It's Christmas tomorrow, ya dancer.'

6

As we approached the end of our street we could see Dot and my ma struggling along with about eight plastic carrier bags each. Dot spotted us before we could escape. 'Hey you two. Come and take these bags up the stair. My arms are falling off.'

A bit of an exaggeration I thought. But if we carried the bags up it was possible that we might get to sample some of the goodies in them. Loaded up like pack rats we were ushered into the close. 'And don't touch a bloody thing. We know every single thing that's in them bags and we will notice anything that's missing,' warned my ma, putting an end to any notion we had of helping ourselves. She was amazing. No matter the number of bags, and the number of items in each bag, she always spotted the slightest discrepancy.

'Where are you going anyway?' I asked, trying to find out if there was anything in this for me. Perhaps they were going to buy Christmas presents.

'To get the housekeeping money from my da and Donald, before they spend it all in the pub or the bookies,' Dot said.

My ma hushed her, 'Don't be saying that in the middle of the street.'

'Well they will spend it all. And we still need to go to the Barras remember. It's nearly three o'clock,' Dot said, in a whisper, with a sidelong glance at Charlie and me.

'When you put thae messages in the kitchen Danny, bump Paul's big pram down the stairs for me son. We need to go a wee message this afternoon,' my ma instructed.

That they needed the big pram to carry stuff back from the Barras could only be good news, I reasoned. With an extra spring in my step

I rushed upstairs with Charlie, leaving my ma and Dot standing at the close having a smoke, trying to find a neighbour to gossip with.

The Barras market in Glasgow's east end is a collection of indoor and outdoor market stalls with an abundance of nooks and crannies and dark corners where goods are bought and sold legitimately, or otherwise. We shouldn't have known about their trip to the Barras because that's where they would be going to get our Christmas toys, and perhaps clothes. If we knew they were going there for presents where did that leave the Santa charade?

It was traditional, and necessary, for poorer Glaswegians to congregate at the Barras as late as possible on Christmas Eve. The stallholders and fly pitchers realised this was their last chance of clearing stock and would sell everything at rock-bottom prices the later it got. It was a game of cat and mouse between the stallholders and potential customers. Both parties would hold out for as long as possible. Then, eventually, midnight arrived and the stallholders surrendered, accepting they had been bested yet again by a worthy adversary – the Glaswegian looking to save money.

Charlie and I eventually managed to get all the bags upstairs, and the pram downstairs. We sat at the kitchen table, exhausted. Darlene skipped in and spied the bags on, and underneath, the table.

'You could put all the messages away, you pair of lazy wee shites,' she observed, pausing only to pull and twist Charlie's ear.

'And you could kiss my smelly arse,' my little brother responded, grabbing the back of her hair. Fortunately for her, Duncan came in the front door just as she let out her first scream.

'Charlie, you wee bastard. Let her hair go and leave her alone. I mean it you wee shite. I'll burst you. Let her go,' Duncan said, as he tried to get between Charlie and the arm-waving, screaming Darlene.

'She just came in and twisted his ear for nothing Dunky. It's her own fault. What does she expect him to do?' I said, trying to avoid the commotion that would be caused by Dunky thumping Charlie. Because then I would have to get involved and I would end up getting thumped as well.

'Leave it the two of you. I'm just back from my work and I'm going back to bed for a wee while,' Duncan said, letting go of Charlie.

He opened the cupboard above the fridge, grabbed a handful of biscuits in one hand, slapped Charlie on the back of the head with the other and then made for the door.

Duncan had left school just four months earlier, aged fourteen, and had already had two jobs. His latest was as a van delivery boy for a furniture warehouse in Bridgeton.

'How come you're home so early anyway?' I asked him.

'Because it's Christmas wee man and I'm going out to get pished,' he replied, grabbing me in a dancing hold and twirling me round.

'You better not. My da nearly killed you the last time. Remember when you came in and were sick over Charlie's bed, and did a piss in the wardrobe,' Darlene rebuked him, in her most petulant tone.

He let me go and grabbed Darlene in a hug. 'Oh beautiful Darlene, my gorgeous little sister. Why don't you do what Charlie suggested and kiss my smelly arse? Mind your own business hen. If you tell my ma or da I'm going out drinking tonight, you won't have any hair left for Charlie to pull,' he promised, then planted a big, wet, kiss on her cheek.

'Beat it you grotty bastard,' was Darlene's ladylike response. 'And anyway, I know somebody that fancies you.'

If anything was capable of stopping Duncan in his tracks it was interest from the opposite sex: 'Do you now, darling Darlene? I think you better spill the beans, baby,' Duncan said, grabbing Darlene and tickling her waist with both hands.

'Get off me you pervert. I'll tell you. Stop tickling me and I'll tell you. Susan Dobie, that's who,' she said, slipping to the opposite side of the table from Duncan.

'Wee no-neck Susie fancies me, does she? She's a boot. But she would be all right for a Christmas ride I suppose,' Duncan laughed as he exited the kitchen.

'That's a terrible thing to say. I'm telling my ma on you as soon as she comes in. You're a bad bastard sometimes Dunky,' was Darlene's understandable response.

Charlie and I had kittens. 'Darlene, have you got any Christmas paper and Sellotape?' I asked, having stopped giggling.

She eyed me suspiciously: 'What for? Why do you want Christmas paper? Have you got a present for your wee girlfriend?'

'I haven't got a girlfriend, wee or big. I need a bit of paper to wrap up presents for my ma and da,' I replied, teasingly, knowing that anything Darlene wasn't aware of annoyed the life out of her.

This aroused her suspicion even more. 'How? Where did you get the money to buy them presents and what have you bought? Let me see them. You're a wee liar. You have not got them anything. You couldn't. Where would you get the money from? You're definitely lying. Let me see them if you're telling the truth then. Go on let me see them, you liar,' she said, all in a single breath.

Darlene quite often refused to let breathing get in the way of talking, with the consequence that she had to speed up the words at the end of sentences as her breath ran out.

'We got them presents,' Charlie said, 'not just him, me as well. We got the money watching people's cars last Saturday when the Rangers game was on.'

As excuses go it was a good one. We lived very close to Ibrox Park, the home of Rangers Football Club. Our street, within walking distance of the stadium, was often used by supporters to park their cars. We had been introduced to a money-making scheme the previous week, by Searcher of course. When the supporters arrived in our street, and got out of their vehicles, we inquired: 'Do you want us to watch your car, mister?'

Innocent as I was I didn't understand the implied threat in this question. If he didn't pay us to watch his car there was every chance that some misfortune would befall it: scratched paintwork or deflated tyres, for example. The normal response from the fans was either, 'Aye, here,' as they handed us five or ten pence, or, 'Aye okay, I'll give you something when I come back.' The latter came from the ones who hoped you wouldn't be there after the game, saving them ten pence.

Our response to those who wouldn't pay up was another veiled threat. 'Well I just hope your motor will be okay until you come back, big man.' This was said in a questioning tone of voice, which usually saw them cough up the ten pence right away. One of the first times I tried this gambit was with a huge man who got out of a scabby old van and was standing beside it tying on his football scarf.

'Can I watch your van for you mister?'

He looked at me, and with a broad Irish accent, said: 'Come here wee chap till I show you something.' He lifted me up. 'Look in the back of the van, son. That's my dog, Rex. He's an Alsatian, an ex police dog. He can run at thirty miles an hour for about an hour, nonstop. He weighs six-and-a-half stone and his bite would take off a gorilla's arm. I will let him watch my van.'

As he was putting me down, Searcher appeared at my back.

'That's a brilliant dog, mister. Really scary. But can he put out fires?'

The big Irishman laughed and gave us ten pence each. 'Little bastards,' he chortled as he walked away, shaking his head.

'I still don't believe you two. Show me the presents and I'll give you a couple of sheets of paper,' Darlene said, still thinking we were having her on.

Charlie glanced at me, and I nodded. His glance and my nod showed our communication was telepathic. His glance posed the questions: should we trust her, can we trust her? If we can then should I go and bring out the presents and let her see them? My nod answered: yes, we can trust her and if it turns out that we shouldn't have then it's my fault.

A glance and a nod translated.

Charlie jumped up and went into the hall cupboard behind the sideboard where the linen was kept. He emerged with a Co-op carrier bag. Darlene's eyes lit up. 'I don't believe you two wee shites actually spent money on somebody else. Wonders will never cease.'

She took the bag from Charlie and cleared a space on the table to spread out the contents. 'Who picked these then?' she asked.

Charlie reverted to the one and only answer to any question he was asked that might lead to blame being allocated.

'It was Danny.'

Darlene looked at me. 'This is beautiful Danny. My ma will love it.'

I blushed. 'It was the best we could find for £1.50.'

'No, I'm being serious Danny. It's really lovely. I bet my ma will have a wee greet when she sees it.'

'It's a plate,' Charlie spat. 'How is she gonny love a plate? What a load of crap.'

Darlene shook her head ruefully. 'It's what it says on it, you wee tadger. Can you no' read? It's a lovely wee poem about the best mum in the world. At least Danny's got some sense and he knows what a nice poem is. No' like you, you wee monster.'

'Aye, you're right. Danny knows all about poems. Cos he's a poof.' Charlie shouted the last four words at me and ran out of the kitchen laughing, banging the door behind him.

As I jumped up to give chase, Darlene said, 'Never mind him Danny. This is really nice. My ma will find it delightful.'

That word was too much for me. 'What are you talking about, you stupid cow? *Delightful*. Do you think you're the Queen of Sheba?'

Darlene turned away sighing, 'I could be. How can you be sure that I'm not? I was probably kidnapped as a wean and dragged here to be brought up with you tramps as a punishment from my wicked stepmother.'

I laughed: 'You're not going to the pantomime you halfwit. Come on, Snow White. Wrap these presents up before my ma comes back.'

My da and Donald came in at seven, clearly having celebrated Christmas Eve with a few liquid refreshments.

'Where's your maw?' my da slurred, as Donald propped him up. 'The wee bastard hasn't left me any dinner out.'

'She did Da, she did,' Darlene assured him, almost in tears. 'I'll heat it up for you. There's some stew and totties from last night. She said I was to heat them up for you when you came in. She did leave your dinner, Da. She did.'

By now she was crying her eyes out.

'Fuck it, I'm not even hungry. I need a drink. Where's that half bottle Donnie?' he grunted, in between drunken burps that could quickly turn to vomit, if past performances were anything to go by.

'I've got it here Da. You sit on the chair at the fire and I'll pour you a drink,' my oldest brother said, gesturing to me to move from the armchair I was sprawled over. I leapt aside like a scalded cat. When my da was this drunk, the best policy was to be out of reach when he lashed out.

He half sat and half fell onto the chair I had barely vacated and mumbled what sounded like: 'Where is the wee bastard? I'll fuckin sort her out. I'm telling you.'

Within ten seconds of collapsing into the chair he was snoring loudly, head on chest. We looked to Donnie for guidance.

What could we do? It was Christmas Eve. My da was steaming and angry at my ma for some reason, or more likely no reason at all, and she could be home any minute.

'What are you all looking at me for? It's Christmas. Cheer the fuck up,' Donnie said, almost but not quite as drunk as my da. 'Has Annie been round tonight?' He looked at us, one after the other, but got no response, so he went on, 'What's the matter with that wee bastard? I'm going to have to sort her out,' before staggering out of the living room. He could have been heading for the bedroom, or more probably the toilet, to spew out some of the excess beer swilling in his stomach.

Darlene turned to me. 'When will my ma be back?'

'How the hell should I know Darlene? She'll be back when she's back.'

Darlene wailed, 'I'm only asking. Don't take it out on me. I haven't done anything have I?' as she stormed out, slamming the living-room door and the door to her bedroom in quick succession.

Charlie came out from his hiding place behind the sofa and grinned: 'See the way my da is sprawled out on that chair. Do you think his money might fall out of his pockets and down the side of the chair?'

'I doubt it Charlie. And if you try to help his money fall out of his pocket, he might wake up and throw you out the window. The only question is: would he take the time to strangle you first?' I replied, in all seriousness.

As usual Charlie took no notice of my warnings and crawled along the floor until he was right beside my da. He gently slipped his hand into Da's jacket pocket and came out with a cigarette lighter and his trademark grin. He whispered, 'Let's have a look through the trouser pockets.' It was said in the style of *Play School*. You know, where the announcer comes out with, 'Let's see what's through the round window.'

My heart was beating rapidly. I was as scared as I could ever remember. Charlie was having the time of his life. He was struggling to suppress his laughter. I don't know whether he was laughing at the look of terror on my face or because of the adrenalin rush that came from what he was attempting, or both.

But he stopped trying to get in the trouser pocket so he could roll around on the floor holding his stomach and pointing at me. But then he was actually sitting astride the arm of the armchair pushing at my da trying to get him on his side for easier access to his trouser pocket, 'Come and help me move him you wee shitebag,' he whispered to me, over his shoulder.

And as I shook my head, Da twitched and mumbled. 'Get a fu ya bassa,' he groaned, waving his arm and knocking Charlie to the floor.

I squealed like a little girl at this and Charlie also found it hilarious. 'Did you hear him Danny? Get a fu ya bassa,' he repeated, laughing uproariously just inches from my da.

'That's a cracker. Get a fu ya bassa.' He continued to roll around, still in stitches. I shook my head and walked out.

'Get a fu then, ya bassa,' was Charlie's cry at my back.

7

Ten thirty at night. I was in the living room lying on the floor beside the couch, watching the television with the sound down so as not to disturb my da. The front door opened and in came my ma, Dot and Annie, Donald's girlfriend, whom he had been going out with since the age of thirteen.

'Oh for Christ's sake, Ma. Look at the state of him. Jesus Christ almighty. It's Christmas Eve as well,' Dot said. She was pointing past me at my da, still sprawled on the armchair, comatose.

Annie asked, 'Do you want a hand going through his pockets Margaret?'

The three women laughed. It was the sort of laugh that said, 'We all know it's true but will laugh as if it isn't.'

'We better try and lift him and get him into his bed,' my ma said. 'Annie, go and get Donnie to help us. He'll be in the bedroom.'

Darlene appeared. 'Aye right. He's every bit as bad as my da. He's lying on the floor of the boys' room with his arse sticking out of his trousers, the manky besom.'

'Och at least it's only his arse, eh Annie,' Dot said. She crossed her legs and exclaimed: 'Oh stop making me laugh. I'm going to pish myself. Oh mammy daddy,' and with that she ran to the toilet.

If you asked me, the three women had enjoyed some Christmas spirit at the Barras. 'Annie, get his other arm and we'll see if we can get him on his feet and walk him ben the room, eh,' my ma said, getting a grip on one of my da's arms with both hands.

As they pulled at an arm each, and tried to drag him out of the chair, Darlene was behind him pushing at his back and saying, 'Da, gonny wake up a wee bit please and get to your bed.'

My da's response was a loud fart and another 'Get a fu ya bassa.'

This was too much for Annie and she let go of the arm she was pulling on: 'Oh Margaret, I have pissed myself. I need to take these drawers aff.' She wiggled out of the room, one hand between her legs, desperately trying to protect her modesty. I could hear Annie and Dot crashing about in the bathroom, shrieking with laughter.

At that my da stood up unaided. 'How can a person have a bloody sleep in this mad bloody house?' before staggering with arms outstretched to his bedroom. He paused just long enough to let off another massive, wet-sounding fart at the door.

Charlie and I could suppress our giggles no longer. We had been behind the couch all this time and, when we giggled, my ma heard us. 'What the hell are you two doing still up? Santa will be here shortly and if you two don't get into bed and straight to sleep, he will go right past this house. Now move. Get to bed, move.'

Any other night we might have tried a token protest but not this time. We were too amused by the loud sound produced by my da's fart. We giggled our way out of the room, but not before my ma grabbed us and pulled us in close. 'My two lovely, handsome boys. Maybe you willny turn out to be drunks as well eh. Look at the pair of you. The handsomest wee boys in Glasgow so you are.'

We enjoyed the adoration for a few seconds before giving out the expected protests when she planted slobbery kisses on our cheeks. 'Go, go, go, and get to bed,' she said. Even at our age we knew the affection was heartfelt.

Charlie was asleep within ten minutes. Yet again, it highlighted the difference between us. He existed on a level where stimulation was all, and if he was being stimulated he was completely there, entirely in the moment. Without stimulation he shut down like a car that had run out of petrol. I was less spontaneous and had to mull over everything I did and everything anybody else did. Sleep would eventually take me but only after I had relived every moment of the day, and re-scripted the bad bits with would haves, should haves, could haves.

I needed a drink. Could I sneak past the living-room door and reach the kitchen for a drink of milk? In fact, I thought that Dunky had left most of a bottle of Irn Bru in the fridge as a hangover cure. I could get it if I was quiet. As I was creeping past the open living-room door, a commando on a mission, I paused, hearing voices.

'Oh my god, how far on are you?' my ma exclaimed.

'I've not had my monthlies since September,' Dot replied, her voice trembling.

I sat down beside the open door and listened. What were they talking about?

'Oh Jesus, Mary and Joseph have you told Anthony?' Annie asked.

'Aye, all he said was, "Right we better get married then before your da or Donnie do me in,"' Dot answered, sighing.

Annie snorted derisively. 'I've always liked Anthony. He's such a thoughtful, romantic, wee bastard! That was a lovely proposal wasn't it?'

My ma giggled. 'Stop it. This isn't funny. What are we going to tell your da?'

'I've told Tony that when he comes round for his Christmas dinner tomorrow, he should say to my da in private that we're thinking of getting married. If he doesn't object we can tell everybody right after the Queen's speech. Nobody needs to know I'm pregnant. If we get married in February or March I might not even be showing,' Dot said, obviously having put some thought into it.

'I will be,' said Annie.

'You will be what, hen?' asked my ma.

'Showing. I will be showing by March. I'm already three months gone. I'm due in June,' Annie sniggered. It sounded more like nervousness than amusement.

'Oh Mother of God,' said my ma. 'What a Christmas Day this is going to be. Two weans on the way. What has Donnie said Annie?'

'He's bought an engagement ring and was planning to ask if he could have a wee engagement party here at Hogmanay. He said he would leave it until the day after Boxing Day before he asked you. So you could get Christmas out of the way.'

Annie hesitated and then blurted out, 'He's gonny ask if I can move in here with you until he can save up a rent deposit. We've got our name down with the corporation housing but they won't offer us anything until we're married and have the wean.' She ended her announcement with her head down, expecting the wrath of my ma.

'Of course you can hen. We'll need to juggle the weans about. But we'll manage,' was my ma's unsurprisingly sensible response.

Dot broke in, 'Where will that leave us Ma? Tony and me were going to ask the same thing. We can't go to his house. There are twelve of them in a two-room-and-kitchen. This house is mad enough but it's a bloody zoo over there. And his ma's always steaming and stinking of her own pish.'

'Dorothy, don't talk about the woman like that. She has a right hard time with big Tony. Any time you see her one of her eyes is black. Ina Dobie told her she should get the doors taken out of her house. They're a bloody health hazard, the number of times she bumps into them.'

The three women smiled, but they didn't laugh. I knew what they were thinking: the doors in their houses were every bit as dangerous.

Unexpectedly, my ma laughed.

'I don't know what's so funny, Ma. My da might throw me out tomorrow if Tony doesn't play his cards right. And he could tell Donnie to bugger off and stay at Annie's house as well for all we know,' Dot said, in a worried tone.

'It's not you two I'm laughing at hen. It's just that I haven't had a period for three months either. But I'm forty-five on my next birthday. I'm sure it's just the change of life with me. But how funny would that be, if we have to tell your da the three of us are pregnant at the same time.'

They laughed. But I don't think any of them found the prospect remotely funny.

8

Four in the morning. Charlie's pulling my arm and shaking me. 'Danny, Danny boy. It's Christmas, get up. Come on. I've looked in the living room. There are hundreds of presents and one of us has got a bike. I think it's you.'

My eyes opened wide despite having had only three hours sleep. The word *bike* had sent a surge of adrenalin through me. I had been pestering my ma for months about getting a chopper. It was the latest craze and I wanted one.

'It's really freezing Charlie. Have you put the fire on in the living room?' I asked, through chattering teeth.

'No way, I'm not putting the electric fire on. My da goes mental when you put it on. You can make the coal fire. I'll help you,' Charlie answered, being unusually intelligent.

'Well let's have a look at what we got first. Then I will make the fire. Okay?' This seemed acceptable to Charlie so I followed his example and put my outdoor jacket on over my vest and pants, which also served as pyjamas. The only footwear within easy reach was my black wellies, so they went on as well.

'It is a bike Charlie. You're right. It is a bike,' I whispered, jumping up and down on the spot, trying not to make a noise. The bicycle had a strand of tinsel tied across the handlebars. It wasn't the chopper I had asked for, but that didn't matter. It was a silver racing bike. It looked new. And it was mine.

Charlie's 'big' toy that year was a Spacehopper, which he immediately jumped on and tried out, almost knocking over the Christmas tree, the display cabinet and me in that order.

'Get off it you eejit. You'll wake up my ma and da.' The order came from Darlene, who was standing in the living-room doorway, rubbing her eyes. 'What time is it anyway? You two shouldn't be up yet. I'm telling my ma.'

Charlie leapt on top of her. 'It's Christmas Darlene and Danny got a new bike, yeeha,' he said, in a quiet shout.

Darlene wanted to continue berating us but Charlie's enthusiasm was infectious and she rushed to the armchair by the window, where her presents were piled high. Mine were on the other armchair and Charlie's and Paul's were at opposite ends of the sofa. Even though Paul was only a few months old he still had a wee pile of presents.

'I've got a Sindy doll, and look, there's a load of new clothes for her as well. They're beautiful Charlie, look,' Darlene gushed.

Charlie looked at her as if she was talking Swahili. 'Has she got boobies?' he asked, trying to pull the dress off Sindy's shoulders.

'Beat it, you wee pervert. You spoil everything,' Darlene said, pushing Charlie away.

'I'm only asking because, look, my Action Man hasn't got a willie. Look,' he insisted, thrusting a trouser-less Action Man in Darlene's face.

Darlene made a noise through gritted teeth that eloquently expressed how irritating Charlie could be when he tried. And try he did, all the time.

We unwrapped everything in a matter of minutes and were delighted with our haul. It included a Mars selection box for each of us. Charlie had opened his and had already eaten the Marathon, the Milky Way and the Spangles. Charlie and I had also got lumberjack jackets, made of thick wool with a checked pattern and a pure-white fur collar. We had dumped our anoraks and put on our new jackets, which didn't quite cover, or match, our grey Y-fronts.

Darlene was busy trying another outfit on Sindy but took the time to say, 'Danny, it's nearly six o'clock. Go and make the fire in the kitchen, and then make this one in here. Charlie can put the kettle on and I'll make the toast. We can take my ma and da their breakfast in bed.'

'Who died and made you the boss?' Charlie responded. Nevertheless he did as he was told and within half an hour both fires were taking hold and there was heat being generated, if you sat close enough to the fire.

Ten minutes later Darlene was standing with a tea tray outside my parents' bedroom door. 'You chap the door Danny, and wake them up.'

Charlie saw the trepidation on my face and said with a loud chuckle, 'Don't Danny. What if he tells you to get a fu ya bassa?'

I joined in with his laughter and within seconds we were on the floor helpless. Darlene was incredulous and kicked both of us as she stepped over our bodies, using her knee simultaneously to knock on the door and push it open. 'Ma, Da, I've made you a cup of tea. It's Christmas,' she announced, in a cheerful voice.

My ma half sat up. 'What time is it hen? And what are thae two halfwits rolling about the floor laughing at?'

'Don't ask me Ma. They're eejits, both of them,' was Darlene's exasperated reply.

My da pulled the blanket over his head. 'Does that fuckin' light need to be on? Somebody shut thae two fuckin' hyenas up.'

We stopped laughing.

'Davie, it's Christmas for god's sake. It's not their fault you've got a hangover. Here, Darlene's made you a cup of tea and a bit of toast. Sit up and get it before I throw it over you,' my ma said, digging her elbow into my da's ribs as she spoke.

'Every day of the year, I get up at six o'clock. You would think that just once I could have a lie in,' my da grumped.

Charlie whispered to me, 'Told you. Get a fu ya bassa,' and we were off again.

When we managed to control ourselves we jumped onto the bed, almost spilling the cup of tea my mother had in her hand. As my da stirred himself, probably to let rip with some more hangover-induced grumpiness, Charlie announced in a high-speed rattle: 'Danny got a bike and a new jacket and I got an orange Spacehopper and a new jacket and a ball. Darlene got some crappy dolls and dolls' clothes. Do you want to see my new ball Da? And Ma, we've got you and my da a present as well. Will we go and get it? Do you want to see it? It's under the tree in the living room. Do you want to see it just now? Do you?'

Even my da wasn't immune to Charlie's enthusiasm. 'Was it a good ball that you got? I might go down to the back court with you and show you how football should be played,' he said, struggling to sit. He lay back against the headboard for support.

'Aye it was a cracker Da. I'll show you,' Charlie said, leaping off the bed. He was running before his feet hit the floor.

The football came hurtling into the bedroom at the same time as his shout of 'catch it Da'. Da didn't catch it. It hit my ma's elbow as she was raising her tea. The cup flew out of her hand, the contents spilling over Darlene and my da. If that had been me, I would have got slapped and locked in my room for a year. But it was Charlie, so my ma and da laughed and my ma said, 'Charlie, watch what you're doing with that ball, son.'

Unbelievable, absolutely unbelievable.

Charlie jumped onto the bed with a wrapped-up gift under each arm. 'Here Ma, Da. We got these for you.'

My da opened his present. 'Five Prince Edward cigars. Excellent boys, well done. They'll do me for after my Christmas dinner.' It didn't matter to him that they were the cheapest of cheap cigars and why should it?

'Danny, this is beautiful son,' my ma said. As predicted by Darlene, she had a tear in her eye.

'It's from both of us Ma,' Charlie chipped in.

My ma pulled him close and kissed his cheek. 'I know it is son. I can see that on the wee tag.' But she looked over his head at me and mouthed the words, 'Thanks Danny. Thank you son.'

'Right come on. Up, up, up all of you. This isn't getting the turkey in the oven or the totties peeled. Come on now, shift yourselves,' my ma said, as my da grabbed Charlie and me and started a wrestling match.

This allowed my ma to get up and put on her housecoat. She turned to us. 'There's a lot to be done. We didn't get much done last night. So you two put your presents in the room and bugger off out for a wee while. Davie, you will need to put the big board on the table and see if Mrs Lamont down the stair will give us a wee lend of her spare chairs. She said the other day she would. There's that many people coming to eat today. I might be better off with five loaves and two fishes than turkey and all the trimmings.'

The big board my ma was talking about was a sheet of industrial plywood about twelve feet long and six feet wide. My da had brought it home from his work weeks before, after my mother complained that she needed a bigger dining table.

'There you go,' he said, as he and Donald struggled to manhandle the board into position on top of the melamine table. They had the added hindrance of Charlie and me trying to help.

We were all gathered in the living room for this event. It was important that we had the necessary facilities for the Christmas and New Year celebrations. A big table was crucial. Previous Christmases had been held at someone else's house. Some of us would be farmed out to uncles or aunties or grandparents, because we had never lived in a house big enough to accommodate us all. This was the first Christmas we would be together for the full day.

My ma touched the corner of the board and it started to slide and topple off the table. My da caught it. 'Don't worry about that hen. I will attach it to the table with a few wee nuts and bolts. Once you put a big tablecloth over it, everybody will think you have a grand big dining table.'

My ma looked at him. He could read her face, as we all could.

'Make up your fuckin' mind Maggie. Do you want to buy a new fuckin' dining table or do you want to have food and fuckin' presents for Christmas?' he raged, kicking the edge of the big board with his steel-toe-capped boot. This caused it to fly up, almost catching Donald on the chin. Donald caught it just in time, preventing any more damage, particularly to the display cabinet that was directly behind him.

A silence descended. Darlene partially broke it by sobbing and running out of the room. Charlie followed behind her. I slid in behind Dorothy and Donald, who was standing with his head bowed. Dorothy was seething. I could see her fists clenching and unclenching, but she said nothing. She had taken the brunt of Da's anger before by sticking up for my ma, and would have been happy to do so again. But she had also learned that saying anything at this point could escalate his anger to a dangerous, even physical, level. So best to let it be and leave my ma to calm him.

Paul, who had been sleeping quietly in his pram in the corner of the room, suddenly started wailing. It put an end to the awkwardness of waiting to see who would speak first.

My ma said, 'Dorothy, go and get him hen. Donald, give your da a hand to fix that board to the table son, will you?'

She was giving my da a choice. We could ignore his outburst, act as if it had never happened, as she was prepared to do, or he could keep it going and we would all suffer the consequences.

There was a pause. You could see my da's mind working. He was trying to find an escape route from the situation that his unwarranted rage had caused without losing face in front of his children. Luckily for us, and especially my ma, he was sober that night.

He chose my ma's option and said, in a hearty tone that none of us believed, but all of us understood: 'Right, that's okay then. This will be fine. I'm telling you.'

Dorothy lifted Paul up and began to soothe him. Donald got an end of the board and stood ready, still not making eye contact with anyone. I slid out of the room to find Charlie and Darlene. Any joy the evening may have held was shattered, broken to smithereens by Da's unexplained, but not uncommon, anger.

But that was weeks before and it had quickly been forgotten. Verbals in our family were forgotten in minutes. Physical fights took hours, or, at the most, days to get over.

In a way he was right. The big board had been screwed to the table and my ma had put three tablecloths on it, which covered it from end to end. It now hung down far enough to make it look like a huge dining table. We knew it wasn't and my ma knew it wasn't, but no-one else would. That was what mattered, not what we knew but what everyone else thought. That was the main thing, and anyway it looked beautiful. Darlene and Dorothy had been delegated the task of setting the table and everything was red: glasses, paper napkins, Christmas crackers.

Charlie and I had declined my ma's instructions to bugger off for a while and get out from underfoot. This was too awesome. We had never seen anything like it. The previous couple of Christmases we had spent with my ma and da at my granny's house in Shettleston. Just Charlie and me with my ma and da. Everybody else went to Uncle Charlie's in Maryhill.

Christmas had been good at my granny's but nothing like this. This was something off the telly. I mean, *napkins*. What was a napkin? At first I thought they were red paper hankies until Darlene called me a philanderer and explained what they were. I think she meant philistine. Darlene had a habit of almost getting words right, but not quite. Years later she would drunkenly accuse her husband of being useless in bed. He didn't know what three-play was.

'Ma, gonny tell them two to get dressed. People are going to start arriving and look at the dirty wee mongrels,' Darlene shouted through to the kitchen.

I looked at Charlie and he looked at me. We were still in our vests, underpants, new fur-collared lumberjack jackets and wellies. Charlie was also wearing his new cowboy hat. 'What is she talking about Charlie? I think we look fine. In fact, I think we look great,' I grinned.

'Go and get dressed you two. Now. Move it. Look at the state of you.' Dorothy had settled it without the intervention of my ma.

Donald walked into the living room with his striped pyjama trousers on and nothing else. He was rubbing the drunken sleep from his eyes and yawning. 'Who's making me a roll and sausage and a mug of tea then? And is Annie here yet?' he asked, looking first at Darlene and then at me.

'Not me anyway.' Darlene got her refusal in first, before I had a chance to open my mouth. 'I'm up to my eyes in napkins and crackers. I'm not making it. Make it yourself or tell Danny. He can make it. And no, Annie isn't here yet.'

I looked around. Charlie was considered too wee to be making tea, but I wasn't. Tea-making was a major part of my reason for existing. My parents must have decided ten years before, 'Do you know what we need? We need to have a wean that can be taught to make tea and then we can make him do it all the time. Every time he walks into a room or walks out of a room or just sits, stands or lies down. In fact, we should put a chair next to the kettle and the teapot and he can pour tea for us and our visitors.'

They should have called me Urnie instead of Danny.

9

Being the family tea-maker was often a source of irritation. But it was Christmas and I was in a good mood. 'Who wants a roll and sausage then?' I asked. Big mistake. 'Me', 'me', 'me', 'me' was the response.

I went into the kitchen, where my ma was enveloped in steam from the array of pots and pans on the cooker. 'Are you not dressed yet Danny? What do you want in here anyway? You're in my way again. Go and get dressed,' she ordered.

'They want me to make them a roll and sausage Ma. Do you want one?' I asked timidly.

'For Christ's sake. Can they not wait for their dinner,' she moaned, wiping her brow. 'You go and get and dressed and I'll clear a wee space. You can do me a wee piece and egg, okay? I need a cup of tea anyway so I do. But go and get something on first. You look stupid in that big jacket and wellies. And go wake Dunky up. He should be helping out as well, the lazy wee shite.'

I was back in the kitchen within a couple of minutes, wearing a pair of school trousers and a woollen pullover. But I spoiled the look by keeping my wellies on.

'Dunky's not in his bed Ma,' I said, digging the frying pan out of the pot cupboard.

'Was he away out early then? You've been up the longest. Did you hear him going out?'

'He probably got lucky at the dancing last night. He was going in to the town with his pals,' Donald said, pushing past me to get his bottle of Irn Bru out of the fridge. 'Which of you wee shites finished my Irn Bru again?' he enquired, poking his fingers into my back.

'Stop it Donald. Where did he say was going? It's not like him to stay out all night. He's only fourteen,' my ma said, obviously concerned.

'I seen him last night sniffing about that wee Susie Dobie,' Dorothy called through from the living room. 'Maybe he's at her house.'

'He better not be. He's only fourteen. Surely her ma and da wouldn't let him stay,' my ma said.

'Danny you nip round to Neilly's. Neilly will know where he is if he isn't there. Thae two are thick as thieves.' Neilly being Dunky's best friend.

'I'm making everybody's breakfast. Send Charlie. He's not doing anything except playing with his balls in the close.'

While I was still sniggering at my deliberate innuendo Charlie came in, breathless and excited. But he still managed to shout, 'The polis are coming up the stair.'

My ma turned white. The rest of us looked at my da. Before he could say anything to allay the fear on our faces there were three loud raps on the door. That was the way the police knocked: three loud raps, everybody knew that. Well, everybody in Glasgow knew that.

'Morning Davie, Donnie,' constable Archibald Brown said. They both knew the cop and he was well aware of them.

'Your other boy, Dunky, is down in the Orkney Street cells this morning. He was boxing up at the Plaza dance hall last night and resisted arrest when we lifted him. He says he's only fourteen. Is that right?'

'Resisting arrest was he Archie? I hope he wasn't trying to hurt your steel-toecap boots with his stomach the way I was the last time you lifted me,' Donald remarked sarcastically.

Archie Brown smiled. 'It's constable Brown to you son.' Then he added, with a smug grin and a glance at his colleague, who also had a sanctimonious smile plastered across his face: 'We were both there, Donnie. You know the score and I know the score. But if you want to come down to Orkney Street, we can discuss it further.'

Donald bridled and took a half step forward. But my da intervened. 'Donald, go and get my boots from the room son. I need to go and get Dunky out, and I've no need to be collecting you as well.'

Constable Brown smirked again. 'Don't be in any hurry. He won't be going anywhere until Monday. The courts are shut. Did nobody tell you it's Christmas?'

His colleague laughed out loud at this, but when he saw my ma's face he cut the laughter off very quickly. He was suddenly uncomfortable, with everybody staring at him through hate-filled eyes.

Brown ignored his colleague's discomfort. 'Because he's only fourteen, we can't keep him in the cells over the weekend.'

My da interrupted. 'Good, I'll come and get him. We'll make sure he stays in the house all weekend and gets to court first thing Monday morning.'

Archie Brown ignored the interruption. 'So he needs to go into a children's home until he is taken to court on Monday.'

My ma gasped and put her hands over her mouth.

'Why would you do that to him at Christmas? That's pure badness. You could have let him out and he would have turned up at court on Monday. Rotten swine that you are,' Dorothy said, in her most embittered tone.

'Be careful miss. Don't use that tone of voice with me or you could be joining him,' Brown's colleague said, again smiling smugly.

Now both Donald and my da moved towards the two constables.

My ma took hold of my da's arm and had her say. 'You've told us what you came to tell us and I'm sure you enjoyed it. It's made your day. But you'll be taking nobody else anywhere today. So away you go back to Orkney Street and torture some other poor soul. Leave us be. Go on you pair of vultures,' and with that she closed the door in their faces.

My da laughed. 'Well that's them told.'

'It's not funny Da. This is our first Christmas here and thae polis bastards have spoiled it. Poor Dunky, in some horrible children's home for Christmas,' Darlene wailed.

'There's no need for that language Darlene. Anyway, Dunky's brought it on himself. Hell mend him. He's not spoiling our Christmas. You two finish setting the table,' my ma said, pointing at Dot and Darlene 'and then come and give me a hand with peeling the totties and vegetables. Danny where's the tea and the piece and egg you promised me?' My ma had taken charge, as usual.

There was another knock at the door. Before anybody could say 'What now?', although most of us thought it, the door opened and Annie came in with two carrier bags, full of Christmas presents.

'What's up Maggie? What were the polis here for? And, oh, Merry

Christmas everybody,' she said, putting the bags down, grabbing Charlie and unsuccessfully trying to give him a kiss and a hug.

'Dunky's got the jail and he's ruined Christmas for everybody. I hate him. I hate him. All he ever does is spoil everything for everybody,' Darlene wailed, slamming shut the bathroom door.

'Apart from that everything's hunky dory sweetheart,' my da said, to general mirth.

I was making the tea and rolls and sausage when Annie, Dot and Darlene came in and sat at the kitchen table with my ma. They obviously thought I was either invisible or deaf.

'What will I do now Ma? My da's probably in a bad mood already and he's opened a can of beer. How am I going to tell him about this?' Dot said, miming a lump over her stomach.

'Are you pregnant Dot? Oh my god. My da will do you in. Oh my god,' Darlene screeched.

Annie laughed. 'For Christ's sake, Darlene. Keep it down. We don't want the whole street to know before we tell your da.' Turning to Dot, she asked, 'Should I tell him about me first? Maybe that will break the ice. He won't start shouting at me, will he?'

Darlene screeched again, putting her hands on the side of her face, 'What do you mean? You as well? Jesus, Mary and Joseph, what have you been doing?'

Annie held her side. 'Stop making me laugh, Darlene. I don't want to pish on your ma's kitchen chair at Christmas. And anyway you know what we've been doing. Or should I tell you about the birds and the bees?'

'Annie, put your hands over Darlene's mouth so I can tell her about my ma being pregnant as well,' Dot giggled.

Darlene was speechless. There's a first time for everything.

'Breathe Darlene,' my ma said. Darlene was staring at her, mouth wide open, not making a sound. 'I might not be pregnant. I might just have started the change,' she went on, directing this to Dot and Annie.

'Do you feel pregnant Ma?' Dot asked.

My ma looked over her shoulder, noticing me for what appeared to be the first time. 'Aye, I would bet my bottom dollar that I'm pregnant again hen. You better breathe as well Danny. And the both of you keep your mouths shut until we work out how to tell your da.'

I must have looked as stunned as Darlene but that was because it had now been three minutes since she had said anything. That was a world record.

My da walked into the kitchen, looked suspiciously at the three women, and Darlene, and said: 'Hubble bubble, toil and trouble. All you four need is a cauldron in front of you. Where are these rolls and sausage Danny boy? I need to put a lining in my stomach before I open another beer. And when you've made them, get through the living room with your brothers. You don't want this lot filling your head with their shite.'

Then, as he opened the fridge to get another beer, he turned to my ma. 'And don't start. It's Christmas. I'm allowed a couple of beers at Christmas. Am I not?'

Ma hadn't said a word.

'Of course you are Davie, but take it easy. I'll be wanting a dance with you after our Christmas dinner and I don't mean me holding you up either. I expect you to be holding me up,' Annie cackled.

'It's just a wee beer or two, hen. I won't have a drop of the hard stuff until after we have our wee dance, okay?' Da took his beer and left the kitchen, glancing at my ma to see if this had mollified her. Perhaps today wouldn't as easy as they had hoped.

'Come and get it then,' Darlene shouted.

'Do you mean dinner is served hen?' my da asked, as he stood up from the armchair and made his way to the head of the table.

As Charlie and I appeared in the doorway that connected the hall with the living room Annie rushed forward and grabbed Charlie. She danced him around, while singing, 'Charlie is my darling, my darling, my darling.' My little brother struggled manfully to escape, although his struggles didn't look genuine to me. A cuddle from Annie was never a bad thing and he knew it. At least that started the meal off in a positive atmosphere.

We all grabbed a chair but Darlene screeched, again, 'Look, before you sit down. Look, I've put place settings out. You're all in the wrong seats. Gonny tell them Ma? It's them two wee jobbies. Gonny tell them Da?'

Charlie and I reached across and swapped Darlene's meticulously thought-out place settings so that everybody's setting was now in front of them.

'There you go. That was easy, wasn't it?' I said.

'It's not the point, Danny. Annie should be sitting opposite Donald and Dot should be sitting opposite Tony. And you and Charlie were supposed to be separate so you can't be a pain,' she insisted, folding her arms in defiance.

'Where is Tony, Dot? Did you not tell him we were going to have our Christmas dinner right after the Queen's speech?' my ma shouted through from the kitchen.

'Aye, I did. But he was going to drop presents into his granny's in Govan before he came here. He's probably sitting getting drunk with them. You know what he's like,' Dorothy explained, reaching for a napkin and tucking it into her top.

The front door opened and Tony stuck his head around the door. 'Sorry, sorry, sorry. My wee granny got gabbing and wouldn't let me leave before I had a wee taste of everything she had made for my granda. Then wee Mary, her neighbour, came in and she wouldn't let me leave until I told her how your move had went and how much you were enjoying this big house. Then she wanted to know what Dot was saying about it and what Annie was saying about it and how are me and Dot not married yet and maybe we should have a double wedding with Donald and Annie, and was my da still in jail, and that must be a heartbreaker for my ma and how was my wee sister coping with the wean? Jesus Christ that woman can talk.' He kissed Dot and moved a chair between her and Charlie so he could squeeze in beside her.

This annoyed Darlene but she settled for a 'harrumph' and an up-and-down movements of her arms, which were still folded across her chest.

'So you didn't have a sneaky wee lager with your granda or a glass of Bristol Cream with your granny?' Dot asked scornfully.

Tony put his arm around her shoulder and pulled her close for a kiss. 'Well, you know me doll. I like to be sociable, hee hee. How you doing Davie? What's all this about Dunky getting a sore face from the polis down at the Plaza last night? I hear the wee man was setting about two of them when that big chancer Archie Brown weighed in with his size twelves.'

'I don't know Tony, but Archie Brown's not long away. He came here to gloat. He's lucky I never threw him down the stairs, him and his glaikit-looking pal,' my da responded, the second can of beer kicking in.

'He's lucky my ma never threw him down the bloody stair,' Dot chuckled.

'Right get your elbows off the table. Here comes the soup,' my ma said, carrying a huge tureen through from the kitchen and putting it in the middle of the table. 'Danny, go and get your bowl. It's on the table in the kitchen.'

I didn't understand. I didn't eat homemade soup. Not since my granny had given us food poisoning when I was five and I ended up in hospital. My relationship with homemade soup ended there and then and I wouldn't reignite that relationship until I was in my mid forties. My wife had made soup, which I felt obliged to eat, yet enjoyed. The only downside was that my missus does catering-size pots of soup, which we have to eat three nights in a row, 'while it's still fresh'.

On the kitchen table was a bowl of Heinz tomato soup. It was for me. I took the bowl through. 'Thanks Ma, my favourite.' It wasn't. Oxtail was my favourite but the fact she had deviated from her strict rules meant a lot. Her normal rule was that you ate what was put in front of you or you didn't eat at all. She must have really liked that wee plate.

The meal progressed the way most meals progressed in my family. You concentrated on eating. If you stopped to get involved in a conversation, you wouldn't get your full share of either the potatoes or the gravy.

If you weren't fast you were last. You ate until you were full and then talked.

10

'Did you enjoy that Da?' Dorothy asked, as he stood up and left the table.

'I did indeed hen. Your ma puts on a good spread. I'm going to loosen the belt on my trousers, sit by the fire and have one of them King Edward's the boys gave me this morning. I'll try to get five minutes peace while the rest of you finish your pudding.'

'I suppose that means I have to go and get the puddings then,' my ma said. She asked Dot and Darlene to come into the kitchen and help bring the puddings through.

'In a minute, Ma. Tony wants to have a wee word with you Da. Just you and him,' Dorothy said. She gestured at Tony to get up and go to my da. Darlene and my ma retreated to the kitchen, not wanting to be part of the next few minutes.

Darlene gave Dot a 'good luck' look as she left. Tony looked shocked that Dot had landed him in it so quickly, despite them having already agreed on a plan. He presumably thought that with the news of Dunky being arrested, Dot might want to postpone his chat with Da, at least for a day or two. So now he stood up, looking ashen, and nervously blurted out, 'N . . . n . . . n . . . no hurry, right Davie? I was wondering if there were any jobs going, with you and Donnie on the roads like.'

Dot was having none of it.

She looked at Tony with unconcealed rage. He wasn't going to wimp out now. 'Aye, but there's that other thing as well Tony. That other really important thing, that we talked about yesterday. There's that as well Tony,' her voice rising to a crescendo, urging him with her facial expressions to man up and get the job done.

'Oh, th . . . th . . . th . . . that,' Tony stammered. 'I th . . . th . . . th . . . thought we might leave that a couple of days.'

'Well think again darling,' Dot said with heavy sarcasm. 'No time like the present.'

My da half turned round in his chair, which was facing the fire, away from Dot and Tony. 'Well whatever it is, spit it out. I'm trying to relax and have this nice wee cigar and you two are getting on my nerves with your bickering. Anybody would think you were married, the way you carry on. Danny, go and get me another can of beer out of the fridge son, will you?'

I didn't want to miss a thing. This was getting interesting. I glanced at Annie, because she and Donnie would be next with their news. Surely they were worried about Tony and Dot putting my da in a bad mood. I couldn't believe it when Donnie said, 'Oh by the way, Da. Annie's expecting. She's due in June. So we thought we would get married in May. She'll be a bit fat by then but never mind, eh?'

This time my da turned fully round: 'Does that mean I'm going to be a granda? Did you hear that Maggie?' he said, raising his voice so my ma could hear from the kitchen. 'We're going to be a granny and granda. Never mind the can of beer Danny. Go and get that bottle of Grouse out of the kitchen press. This calls for a half. Hee hee. Donnie's going to be a da. You'll know all about it now son. That's you skint for the next twenty years. Maggie come through here and have a wee half. We need to celebrate.'

He stood up and approached Annie, who remained seated at the table. Smiling, he said, 'How far on are you hen? You're not showing yet. Are you sure?' This last part was put while looking directly at Donnie.

I was too young to realise it but that question, in his mind, probably meant, 'Are you sure it's yours, son?'

Annie picked up on the implication and came straight back at Da. 'Aye we're sure. I've been to the doctors and I'm three months gone. And *we* are very happy about it.'

The emphasis on *we* was deliberate.

My da backtracked. 'Oh that's great. I remember your ma falling pregnant with Donnie. I was shit scared to tell her da. I hadn't even met him. Your ma and I did all our courting without anybody in her family knowing, what with her being a Catholic and me a Proddie. No' that that matters. We were never ones for church or chapel, but Granda Paul was. He was a nice-enough man, but fierce for the chapel.'

As he said this my ma and Darlene came back in: Darlene with a big bowl of trifle and my ma with a Christmas pudding.

Dorothy was raging. She was raging with Donnie for nipping in and getting his news in first. She was raging with Tony for wimping out. And she was raging with everybody else for . . . well, I don't know what for. Probably for being there.

And then Tony, maybe thinking he could pacify her, exclaimed, 'Oh man, that's brilliant. We should have a double wedding.'

Donnie laughed, while my da turned to Tony.

'What did you say Anthony?' he asked, ominously using Tony's full name.

Tony knew, as we did, that when my ma or my da used your Sunday name, what followed was not going to be pretty.

'You dirty wee bastard. Have you got my wee lassie pregnant?' Da growled.

Without further ado he launched himself at Tony, punching him to the floor.

Pandemonium ensued. My da had fallen when he hit Tony and was now rolling about trying to land another punch or a kick. In the meantime Darlene had thrown the trifle onto the table and jumped on my da's back.

She was crying. 'Don't hit him Da. Don't hit him.'

My ma sat down at the table. 'Oh for Christ's sake, it's Christmas. Just one day for Christ's sake. Can we have one happy bloody day?'

Donald and Annie did their best to pacify my da. At one point Annie said, 'Davie, stop throwing punches. You might hit me and I'm pregnant. Just calm down and let him speak.' She was gesturing towards Tony, who had crawled away and was now standing in the hall, peering round the door. He was ready to bolt from the house at the first sign of my da getting loose.

It didn't occur to anyone that Tony hadn't said Dot was pregnant, only that they could have a double wedding. It had been taken for granted she was pregnant. Why else get married at seventeen?

I burst out laughing. My da whipped round to look at me. I was going to get it next. But he had to snigger when I pointed at what had made me laugh. Charlie was sitting at the dining table with two spoons, eating the trifle that Darlene had spilled. His face was covered in cream and the front of his pullover was dripping with jelly and custard.

When he realised we were all looking he asked: 'What, what's the matter? There's no use letting it go to waste, is there? It's Christmas trifle.' He continued to eat two-handed.

By seven that evening my da had more or less calmed down. Dot had stormed off to her bedroom raging at the world while Tony had spent the next half an hour knocking on her door and pleading to be let in.

Tony also had to suffer my da's constant sniping, remarks like, 'You would be as well letting him in. What worse harm can he do now?' and 'What kind of man whines like that for god's sake?'

Poor Tony. There was no respite, what with Dorothy periodically screaming at him, 'Go away. You couldn't even stand up for me. Go away. I hate you.'

When my da or Donnie went to the toilet, or for another beer, they would continue with the sarcasm. 'Don't let her talk to you like that. Sort her out.'

If it was my da speaking Tony would flinch, put his hand up to his swollen eye and check that his path to the front door was clear. If my da moved towards him he could bolt.

And then Charlie and I would repeatedly break into a chorus of 'I'm getting married in the morning'. This was much to Darlene and Dot's displeasure and they would repeatedly shout, 'Ma, gonny tell them to leave Tony alone. They are being wee shites again.' No sense of humour these people. None at all.

By ten, Donnie, my da and Tony had polished off the lion's share of the Grouse. Now, in the merry stage of drunkenness, Tony was being hailed as a brother and a son. The three of them confidently predicted that the two women would produce strapping sons, that they would be best pals forever and that the two boys would do all the things they hadn't been capable of doing.

Those boys would not only play for Rangers or Celtic – Tony was a Celtic fan – but would also score the winning goal for Scotland in the World Cup final. England won a World Cup, and we beat them all the time, so it was only a matter of time before Scotland won it too. If football wasn't the kids' future they would be lawyers or doctors. These two sons, and grandsons, would to be the best at whatever they chose to do. Goes without saying.

Prudently, Dorothy coaxed Tony away from my da before the merry stage of drinking passed and was replaced by the fighting stage. Because Tony was no longer there to fight with, Donald and my da settled for reminiscing about past altercations, of which there had been many.

11

Christmas Day 1970 was over. I spent Boxing Day out on my new bike with Charlie, Searcher and Bobby. Searcher's Christmas presents had been a selection box and a new, at least to him, winter coat.

Bobby's gift was a black eye from his ma's latest boyfriend. He was always at a loss to explain why his mother had so many boyfriends when she was almost permanently drunk and rarely left the house. But there had been plenty of them, and more than a few had lashed out at Bobby when drunk. He wouldn't have to suffer it for much longer though. We put a stop to all that a couple of years later.

We didn't do much that day. It was too cold, even for mischief. The one memorable thing was bumping into a boy I knew from school, Mirza Chandra. His father was a Sri Lankan immigrant, but he had been born in the city and spoke with a Glaswegian accent as broad as mine. We only noticed him because he was riding a brand-new Chopper. It was red and it was beautiful.

I had Charlie on the handlebars of my bike and Searcher had Bobby on the back of his. With Bobby the Bear to cope with, Searcher's little legs had to move like pistons to get the bike moving. And it was only by Bobby putting his feet on the ground that he could get it to stop.

'Danny, check out the Chopper that wee Paki's on,' Searcher called out, as he spotted Mirza on Paisley Road West, which crossed the top of our street.

We sped over to have a better look at the bike and who was riding it. When the boy heard us I shouted, 'Mirza, you fat bastard. Where did you get the Chopper?'

He slammed on his brakes. 'I got it for my Christmas, you wee dwarf.'

Charlie bristled at the insult, not taking into account that I had called Mirza a fat bastard.

I ignored what Mirza had said. 'How come? You don't believe in Jesus. How come you get a Christmas present?'

'Well you don't believe in the Easter bunny. But you still get a fucking Easter egg, don't you?' was his logical reply.

Bobby had dismounted from Searcher's bike and was circling Mirza menacingly: 'This is a cracker of a bike. It's a beauty all right.' He turned to Searcher and said, in his most chilling tone: 'We could just take it off him Searcher. You should have a bike like this.'

We were at a crossroads, a crossroads that could affect the rest of our lives. Stealing a bike was serious stuff. Searcher sensed how important this moment was. He looked at Charlie, then me. The look on our faces said it all: we weren't going to steal the bike. And we weren't going to stand by and watch Searcher and the Bear steal it either.

Mirza wasn't a friend of mine. He was somebody whose name I knew, somebody from school. We didn't have a Chopper, and we would have loved one. But stealing one from him would have made me sick.

Searcher got that, instantly. He was the most streetwise kid I had ever met. An order was barked to Bobby.

'Don't be stupid. That's Danny's pal. He's an all-right wee Paki. Leave him alone. But you could let us have a wee shot on it wee man. Just to the end of the street and back, eh?'

We passed a couple of hours up and down the street on Mirza's bike, so engrossed that I missed my ma breaking the news to my da that she too might be with child. By the time I went home, my da had decided this was another cause for him and Donald to celebrate. Three future Scotland players would be born into the clan McCallister in 1971. Funnily enough, all three children would be boys. None of them ever played for Scotland.

Dunky got a £10 fine and was let out of the children's home the day after Boxing Day. I could hardly stop laughing when Darlene and I regaled him with a rundown of our Christmas Day. The tale included my da punching Tony and then treating him like the prodigal son when he was drunk. And Charlie scoffing most of a trifle made for eight people.

When I mentioned the episode with Searcher and Mirza, making sure that I could rely on him if anything like it occurred again, he said, 'Watch them two Danny. It's okay them being your pals. But they are not your brothers. They will both end up in the jail if they're not careful. Don't you or the wee man be with them when they do.'

Dunky didn't see the irony considering where he had been over Christmas. But he would, many years later, prove to be right.

Nevertheless, I should have taken his advice.

12

The next few days, between Christmas and New Year, were again spent in a frenzy of cleaning and cooking. My ma would make several large steak pies, which would be squeezed into the fridge awaiting the bells at Hogmanay. She would also make at least one, sometimes two, clootie dumplings.

That was a sight to behold. All the ingredients for the dumplings went into a pillow case and then into a giant pot to steam for what seemed to be hours on end. She made fruitcake, black bun and shortbread as well, but these were now affordable, from the Co-op in Govan, and especially if your daughter's fiancé worked in the warehouse.

In our house at Christmas there were no rituals, religious or otherwise. But Hogmanay had loads, all of which had to be strictly adhered to in order to avoid bad luck for the rest of the year. The whole house had to be clean and all bags of rubbish taken down to the bin before the Bells. More importantly, no one should partake of alcohol before the Bells.

The list went on. Immediately after the Bells everyone had to sit down for steak pie and totties. No other meal would do. Then there was the tradition of the 'first-foot'. It wasn't considered safe to leave the house until you were 'first-footed'. Almost anyone would have done; a friend, a neighbour or even a stranger. Of course, that someone should if at all possible be tall, dark and handsome.

To get round the rules I would, on occasion, be exiled to the landing outside our front door at one minute to midnight and told to knock on the door after the Bells. My ma's reasoning being that two out of three wasn't bad: I was dark and handsome, if not too tall, at least according to her. When I was exiled it was imperative that my arms should be filled with the things that would guarantee luck in our house in the year ahead. Things like a lump of coal, salt, a drink – preferably whisky – a bit of black bun and shortbread.

It was also a tradition that as the first foot, and once I had handed over the gifts, I would be plied with food and drink. Still too young for booze, I would get a fruit cordial, which seemed to be on sale only at the New Year.

Hogmanay plays an important part in my memories. It would play host to three engagements, two arrests, a birth, a death and several fistfights that resulted in long- and short-term fall outs. Hogmanay 1970, however, was one of the happiest I can remember. I was under the kitchen table lying down, reading a book. It was one of the warmest spots in the house and not too terrible a place for keeping an inquisitive mind up to speed with what was going on.

'Ma, what can I wear tonight? I feel as if my belly's sticking out the top of these hot pants. I canny wear them,' Dorothy complained, as she walked into the kitchen trying to fasten the front button on a pair of yellow hot pants. Her stomach was hanging out of the space between the top of her hot pants and the bottom edge of her crop top.

I covered my mouth to suppress my mirth. I could come out of this very badly by laughing at an inappropriate moment.

'I don't have a bloody clue why you would want to wear them stupid-looking things anyway. What do you think you look like with a pair of shorts, half a bloody blouse and platform boots on? You look bloody ridiculous. Go and look in my wardrobe. There's a nice midi-dress you can wear, the mint-green one with the tie belt. Try that on.'

'Oh Ma, midis are out. Maxis are in. I'm going to see if I can get a loan of Annie's maxi-dress; at least that should fit me. I can wear my flat shoes with it instead of these boots,' she said, tottering out of the kitchen.

Within a minute we heard shouting: 'No. If I can't wear them neither can you, Darlene. Get thae hot pants down, you skinny wee bitch.'

'Ha ha. Is that what Tony said to you?' Darlene responded, running into the kitchen and behind my ma for protection, hot pants in hand.

'Ma, gonny tell her she's not wearing my clothes. I'll still want them after I have this wean,' Dorothy said, deeply unhappy about not being able to fit into her clothes.

'Well you're not going to have the wean before the Bells. So let her wear them just for tonight. What harm is there in that?' my ma suggested, in her most diplomatic tone.

'If you get as much as one stain or one tear in them, I will kill you Darlene. I mean it. I saved up for weeks for thae hot pants and I put them away for tonight. One bloody stain and I'll kill you,' Dorothy spat at Darlene.

'You'll not fit into them after you have the wean. You had a fat-enough arse before you got pregnant,' Darlene retorted, her mouth taking control of her brain again.

'That's it. Give me them back you bitch,' Dot said, trying to reach around my ma and slap Darlene, but succeeding only in irritating her even more.

'Sit down! Both of you,' my ma shouted. 'For god's sake, as if we don't have enough fighting with all the idiotic men in this house without you two starting as well. Darlene, don't be so bloody cheeky to your sister. Say you're sorry.'

Darlene had a petted lip. She often let her mouth rule her head and would never admit what she had said was wrong. Darlene didn't sit down. She sidled her way to the kitchen door and gave her parting shot, before sprinting into her bedroom and locking the door.

'Okay Ma. I'm sorry. I'm sorry that Dorothy has got a big fat arse.'

13

I'm not sure how, but my ma eventually got them to declare a truce. They spent the rest of the evening happily blow-drying each other's hair and swapping make up.

'Hello there Maggie. All ready for the Bells then?' Tony asked, exploding into the kitchen in that unique way of his. He was wearing faded jeans, a tie-dyed shirt and had his hair in a ponytail.

Dunky, who was at the kitchen table cutting his toenails, exclaimed, 'Oh look. It's the hippy-hippy-shake man. What are you supposed to be? Are you going to San Francisco, or what?'

Tony was affronted. 'I look cool. Not like you, you wee tramp.'

Dunky was out of his chair and up and at Tony before he could blink. But it was in jest and Tony pretend-wrestled him to the floor. Dunky was giggling: 'I might be a tramp but at least I don't look like a big poof triple T.'

'Mind your language Duncan, There's no need for that. And what is that supposed to mean, triple T?' my ma enquired, passing the kitchen door.

'It's his new nickname. Touch your toes for Tony,' Dunky said, rolling away behind my ma before Tony could renew his grip on him.

'That's disgusting. Don't you say that again,' my ma ordered, swiping at Dunky with her hand and missing him as he ducked away laughing.

Tony ignored him and gestured me closer to him, half-whispering: 'Is your da in and is he drunk?'

'Aye, he's in the living room and he's not drunk. My ma won't let him have a whisky till after the bells,' I replied defensively.

'Oh, aye, right. Where is Dot then?' he asked in a conspiratorial tone.

'She's in the bathroom, with Darlene, putting their make up on. Why?' I asked, wondering what he was up to.

He winked. 'Are you going to be the first foot again?'

'I don't know, do I? If my ma tells me I am then I am. Why?' I said, intrigued.

'Here, put this in your pocket. And when you come in with the black bun and coal and that, give it to Dot,' he grinned. It was a ring box.

'What for? How can you not give it to her?'

'Because when you give it to her I'm going to propose. It will be romantic,' he said, still grinning.

'It will be stupid you mean. She will think it's me that wants to marry her. I don't. She's nice enough I suppose, apart from her big fat arse. But I don't want to marry her.'

He slapped me gently on the side of the head. 'Don't be cheeky about your sister and do as you're told. I'll give you fifty pence tomorrow.'

Charlie, who had been standing listening to this exchange, had to intervene. 'Do you think he buttons up the back Tony? Give him the fifty pence now or else he gets to keep the ring. By tomorrow you won't remember if it's New Year or New York.'

Charlie took the ring box from my hand and looked inside, adding, 'In fact, give him the fifty pence now. He doesn't want to keep the ring. It's not even worth fifty pence. It's brass.'

Tony clipped Charlie round the ear and snatched the ring box back, handing it to me as he fished in his pocket. He gave me a load of loose change, which added up to sixty-four pence. 'You two think you're Morecambe and Wise, don't you? A right wee double act. Well you're not funny. That ring cost me twelve pound out of the pawn, and it better bloody fit her.'

Charlie couldn't resist it. 'Aye, well as long as her fingers aren't as fat as her arse you've got a chance, big man.' Even Tony laughed at that one, but he did look over his shoulder first to make sure Dorothy wasn't in earshot.

Twenty minutes to midnight, Darlene and Dot appeared in the living room. Everybody else is already there. The men are staring at the television watching, 'Ring out the old and bring in the new'. It was similar to *The White Heather Club*, a load of teuchters in kilts prancing about and talking indecipherable shite. In these festive programmes they were all so nicey nice to each other. It was nothing like Hogmanay in Glasgow. Not one of them got head butted or was sick behind a couch.

Charlie and I were helping my ma set the table for the steak-pie dinner and putting out the sausage rolls and sandwiches for the guests who would come in later. Charlie's philosophy with sausage rolls was one for me and one for you. My ma twice told him off for eating more than he was putting out.

Dorothy gives a discreet cough, hoping Tony will turn round and see her in all her finery. She had borrowed a maxi dress from Annie and looked lovely.

'Look at the state of these teuchters dancing, Davie. If I swung Dorothy round like that she would be vomiting out of the window after two minutes,' Tony said, with immaculate timing, to his prospective father-in-law.

Darlene tried a polite cough. Getting no response, she took the bull by the horns: 'That's us ready for the New Year. Bring on the Bells,' she said, spinning round and giggling.

At last Tony turned round. But when he spoke it was to Darlene, not Dorothy. 'You look absolutely gorgeous darling. You really suit thae hot pants.'

My ma was stunned. She sat down at the table and put her head in her hands. My da, Donnie and Dunky laughed. Perhaps if Tony hadn't turned back to inquire what they were laughing at he would have seen Dorothy's fist coming and it wouldn't have blackened the eye that my dad had missed the week before.

When the furore died down, Dot was dispatched to the bedroom with Darlene to fix her mascara. My da said she looked like a panda, which didn't help. I went into the coal bunker, got a lump of coal and picked up a can of beer. I was heading for the shortbread when my ma said, 'You don't need to first-foot, Danny. Big Ronald MacDonald from across the road said he is coming over right after the Bells.'

Tony, who was now holding a few slices of square sausage on his eye – we couldn't afford steak – said, 'No Maggie. Will you let Danny first foot? He's doing me a wee favour.'

She shook her head and said, sternly, 'What wee favour?' I think she had had enough of Tony's capacity for disaster for one night.

He explained his proposal plan and Ma asked, 'Will she not think Danny's proposing to her if he gives her the ring?'

I thought about how I could get the fat arse joke in, without saying 'arse' in front of my ma. But before I could say anything, Tony asked, 'What's the matter with this family? Have none of you got any romance in your soul?'

My ma looked at me, my da, Donnie, then Dunky. And then we all looked at each other and gleefully said in unison, 'No!'

Poor Tony, his head leaning back so the square sausage wouldn't fall off his eye, didn't see the funny side.

It was now two minutes to midnight and just as I went towards the front door it burst open. Annie came running in. 'Get out of my way, I need a pee. Move it or I'll pee in the hall. Oh mammy daddy I mean it.' She was in the bathroom and peeing within three seconds, the door wide open. She let out a cackle. 'You can shut this door if you like Maggie. I don't want to frighten the weans.'

I stood outside in the close wishing I had put a coat on. It was freezing. I heard a ship's horn blow its low, low note. We lived close enough to the docks to hear ships sounding their whistles and horns at midnight on Hogmanay, another Glasgow tradition. We heard the churches ringing their bells, another tradition, one that led to midnight being called the Bells.

I could also hear my family counting down, along with the teuchters on the telly: '. . . five, four, three, two, one and a Happy New Year,' they shouted at the tops of their voices. They sang 'Auld Lang Syne' in time with the teuchters, and then I could hear them wishing one another Happy New Year. Every male in the house had to shake hands with every other male, including baby Paul, and kiss every woman. It was yet another tradition.

Apparently, it wasn't a tradition to let the first foot in before he froze his bollocks off.

Eventually I got in and went through the ritual of handing over the coal, salt and shortbread to my ma and the drink and bit of black bun to my da. Then everybody lined up either to shake my hand, the men, or kiss me, the women.

And when that was over I went to the pram in the corner and bent over to kiss wee Paul. But Tony jabbed his finger in my back and gestured towards Dot with his head, still holding the square sausage over his eye.

I remembered what the plan was and what was in my pocket. 'Oh aye, I forgot. Sorry.' I went over to Dot, who was sitting with Annie, crying, complaining to her about how the evening had gone.

I couldn't remember. Did he want me to go down on one knee and hand over the ring? Or was I supposed to say something when I handed it over? I couldn't remember so I threw the ring box in her lap and said 'here'.

She picked it up and looked at me, puzzled. No wonder. Why would I give her a ring box? Tony is definitely an idiot, I thought. And to prove my point Tony tried to leap over the arm of the chair Dorothy was sitting on, presumably intending to end up on one knee in front of her. But his acrobatic manoeuvre went spectacularly wrong. He caught his knee on the back of her head and fell at her feet. The tie-dyed shirt was now halfway up his back, revealing a layer of grime.

There was a good reason for him being manky. When he had finished work at the Co-op warehouse, the baths on Summerton Road were shut. Like many people at the time, he didn't have an inside toilet or bathroom so he hadn't been able to have a wash.

'What the hell are you doing Tony?' Dot asked, rubbing her head with one hand and holding on to the ring box with the other.

Tony twisted round till he was facing her. 'That's from me,' he said, pointing at the ring. 'Will you marry me Dorothy McCallister?' he grinned, somehow managing to keep the square sausage over his eye.

Dorothy dropped to her knees, straddling him, and kissed him full on the mouth. 'Aye, I suppose so.'

'Right you two. There's weans in here. Cut it out,' Annie said. She obviously wanted a proposal like the one we had just witnessed. 'That was really romantic, Donnie. How come you haven't went down on one knee and asked for my hand in marriage?'

Donnie was embarrassed. 'You told me you were pregnant. I told you we better get married. What was wrong with that? Was that not romantic? I could have done a runner you know.' Then he reached for his can of lager.

Annie smiled, well just about.

14

Taking into consideration this was our first Hogmanay in a new house, a lot of people were there. We had an open-door policy at the New Year, as did most Glaswegians. Most of those who crossed our door-step were neighbours and we would become close to many of them.

Searcher turned up with his da, who would become a good friend to the McCallister family. With his stall at the Barras, and all his contacts there, he was a good man to know. In fact, if you liked a bargain, and weren't fussy about its origins, he was a great man to know.

Bobby turned up but without his mother or her latest squeeze. They had both passed out before midnight. As he pointed out, they didn't need the excuse of Hogmanay. My ma took to Bobby straight away. She treated him like one of her own from the first minute she met him. For all his size and clumsiness he was clearly a little boy lost, a child in need of love, and that she had in abundance.

I counted three, but Dunky said it was four different girls he walked home from our house that night – and the following morning. One of them was Ina Watson. The Watsons would eventually become our nemesis. Their family was similar in size and age groups to ours. There were six brothers and three sisters; although we would later find out that the baby of the family was the child of the oldest sister, who had her when she was only twelve. Mother Watson claimed the child as her own and no one discovered the truth until many years later.

Ina Watson wasn't a pretty girl. That didn't concern Dunky. His philosophy when it came to women was that there was no need to look at the mantelpiece when you were poking the fire. He walked her home at two in the morning. This was very early, but she was working the next day as a cleaner at the Southern General in Govan. When he got back he was in the kitchen with four or five women gathered around him, including my ma and Dot. I was curious. Surely he wasn't revealing details of his tryst with Ina Watson.

'Anyway, there she was. Lying in a corner behind the couch grunting like a maddy,' Dunky laughed. Everybody else in the room was either dancing or drinking, or both. It was mental.'

Darlene moved towards the periphery of the group, eager not to miss a good story. 'What are you talking about Dunky? What was mental?'

'I'm just telling my ma what happened when I walked Ina Watson back to her house. When we got up there the party was in full swing. There were as many people there as there are here. But they were mostly jakies. It was all cheap bottles of wine, and two packets of crisps between thirty of them. Anyway, she invites me in and I'm sitting on a manky old couch between an old man and woman, who turn out to be Ina's ma and da. They looked about eighty but I think they're about the same age as you Ma,' he said, pausing only to munch on a sausage roll, which he had put inside a ham sandwich.

'I'm just sitting there thinking: "How long do I have to stay in this dump to make it look like I'm not just bolting?" Do you know what I mean? I was trying not to be cheeky, but the place was minging.'

'Then I heard something behind the couch. It sounded like somebody greeting. I had a wee look over the back of the couch and there was a fat lassie, lying on her back, howling. She was getting louder. So I said to Mrs Watson, "Is she all right?" And do you know what she said to me?' he asked, an incredulous look on his face.

"Aye son, she's hunky dory. She's just having a wean."'

Dunky by now had a captive audience. 'I nearly shat myself. Sorry Ma. And I said, "What do you mean? Do you mean she's pregnant or that she's actually having the wean right this minute?"'

'Mrs Watson said: "Don't worry son. It's my young sister. This is her fifth wean. She'll be fine. It's like shelling peas when you've had that many."'

'I was definitely ready to bolt now. These people were mental. I asked Mrs Watson, "Should you no' get an ambulance or something or at least find a doctor?"'

'She took another mouthful of her Old England cheap wine, out of the bottle I might add, and said, and you won't believe this, but she said, "We told her to get an ambulance but she said she wasn't ruining her New Year. She wanted a drink and a dance and no wee bastard was going to spoil it for her, so just leave her be. She'll be brand new. She's happy where she is."

'So anyway I looks back over the couch and she's grunting like a big fat pig and her legs are wide open and her dress is up round her belly and I can see her . . . her . . . her . . . .'

He glanced at my ma, unable to think of an appropriate word: 'Well I can see everything, and listen to this: I could see a wean's head, just the top bit, a wee hairy head coming out of her . . . her . . . her . . . .

'Well, just coming out of her. It was mental. So I start jumping up and down, saying to Mrs Watson, "Help her. Look, that's a wean coming out of her. Somebody better help her, for fuck's sake."'

'Sorry Ma.'

'I was shouting, "Don't just sit there. Give her a hand."'

'And Mrs Watson says, "Of course it's a wean coming out of her. What did you expect, a monkey?" And they all start laughing.'

'That was enough for me. I bolted for the door and, as I was leaving, I said: "That's not right. That's what animals do. There's something up with you lot."

'I ran home as fast as I could. Three of the Watson boys were looking daggers at me. I think they'll come after me if they get the chance,' he said, puffing his chest out.

'Was it a boy or a lassie?' Darlene asked.

Dunky looked at her astonished. 'How the hell would I know? I only seen its head. Whatever it was, it's in for some life I'll tell you that for nothing. They were no better than animals.'

Dunky didn't recognise irony when he saw it. He didn't mention he had sex with Ina Watson in the midden area of their back court before he went up to the Watsons' house that night. But it was only them that acted just like animals, wasn't it?

We heard later that day from another neighbour that it was Betty Watson's sister, Morag Mackenzie, who had given birth in her sister's living room. She now had a remarkably healthy baby boy, weighing six pounds eight ounces. Because no one wanted to cut the umbilical cord, she had lain there attached to her baby for four hours, until someone had phoned a taxi to take her home.

However, the driver, who happened to be black, decided it would probably be better to take the drunk woman with a baby attached to the hospital, rather than home to Penilee. Morag was calling the baby 'Winston', after the taxi driver.

New Year's Day was a strange one in our house. It was the same all over Glasgow. The party had finished at first light, roughly nine o'clock. There were always stragglers, no matter where you went.

Darlene found a young girl aged about twenty in a drunken slumber under her bed and left her there to sleep it off, figuring she was safer there than wandering the streets drunk. There were also two friends of Donnie sitting at the kitchen table asleep. Annie woke them up and told them it was time to go home. They protested mildly, probably because they were tired. They must have been shattered because when I saw them in our back close at eleven o'clock they were still knocking out the zeds.

15

The first of January was strange because almost everybody was asleep until late afternoon. In consequence, the normally bustling Paisley Road West was a ghost town. It was deserted. The buses weren't running and the only shop that was open was Mr Ali's, and only for a couple of hours.

It was however a good day for exploring, at least according to Searcher. He woke me up just after ten; I had managed all of two hours' sleep. His suggestion was that we should take a wee bike ride along to the Bellahouston hotel, and then over the new footbridge that crossed the as-yet unfinished M8 motorway, to the Sherbrooke hotel.

Apparently, at this time in the morning, the cleaners dumped the rubbish from the function suites into the skips behind the hotels. This was treasure trove, he informed me. The cleaners swept everything up, bagged and binned it. In previous years he had found wallets and purses and there were always numerous pairs of shoes and lots of unopened or unfinished bottles of booze. Last year he had found two bottles of Champagne. When I asked why the cleaners didn't help themselves, he told me they used to until one of them got the sack for it.

So off we went; Searcher, Charlie and me. Searcher couldn't rouse Bobby. There was no one answering at his house. In fact he only managed to wake us up because our front door was still open. He didn't wake Charlie up, just me, but the wee man had a sixth sense. When I woke up, he woke up. He was harder to avoid than nits.

Searcher forgot to mention a couple of things. For example, to get into the skip at the back of the Sherbrooke, we had to climb an eight-foot-high wall that had barbed wire along the top. We eventually managed to get over the wall using planks of wood from nearby scaffolding, but when I caught a whiff of the rotten food in the skip, I point blank refused to get into it.

We found a solution. Searcher and Charlie would go into the skip and throw out any promising-looking bags. I would then thoroughly search them for anything worth keeping.

After an hour of hard work we had built up a little pile of goodies. We had about £1.40 in coins, at least ten half-full bottles of wine – we knew at least twenty people who would buy them – a pair of high-heeled shoes, a load of unused party hats and one new-looking bra.

There was also a black bag that hadn't been opened, full of little bars of soap and sachets of shampoo. We surmised that it had been either thrown out by mistake or that one of the cleaners had stashed it, intending to return later.

All of a sudden, I heard a screeching noise behind me. When I turned round I saw a boy and a girl, about the same age as me, opening a gate in the wall that we had struggled to get over an hour before. They didn't see me as they wandered towards the side door and entered the hotel. Maybe they were staying at the hotel, maybe not. They left the gate open. That was going to make it easier for us to get our haul away.

We scavenged for another ten minutes before calling it a day. It would be hard enough to carry what we already had. We were outside the gate the boy and girl had gone through, trying to tie four carrier bags to the handlebars of two bikes, when they emerged from the hotel. The girl, who was about Charlie's age, quickly stuffed something inside her coat when she saw me looking at her.

'What have you got there, hen?' I asked.

'Nothing,' she said shyly, keeping her hand inside her coat.

'Let me see then if it's nothing,' I replied, walking across to her.

The boy looked around furtively: 'Don't show him anything Patricia. Come on, let's go,' he instructed.

But she hesitated. 'I'll show you but it's mine and you're not getting any of it.' She looked so determined. We were left in no doubt that whatever it was, she was keeping it.

'Okay, just let me see,' I told her.

She opened the coat and in her hand was a bundle of cash. It looked like £5 and £10 notes.

'For fuck's sake. Where did you get that?' I spluttered.

'Found it and it's mine,' she insisted, once again with *that* look on her face. It said, 'Try to take this at your peril.'

Charlie was hovering, trying to see what she had in her hand. 'What is it she's got Danny?'

I turned to him and Searcher. 'It looks like £5 notes.'

This was big trouble. I wanted nothing to do with the bundle of cash. They had obviously stolen it. 'Right, Searcher. You give Charlie a backie on your bike and I'll take the bags on mine.'

The girl took this as her cue to walk away. I asked, 'What will you do with that?'

She sauntered away. Looking back, she shrugged her shoulders. 'Buy new shoes probably.' As she spoke she gave me the most beautiful smile imaginable. I was too young fully to enjoy that smile.

But I got a wonderful glimpse of the future.

16

The day after New Year's Day, the second of January 1971, there was a huge game at Ibrox. It was Rangers versus Celtic. That meant loads of money, according to Searcher. This would be my first experience of the Old Firm, the biggest derby in the world. An exciting prospect for a kid my age.

Our first port of call was at the bottom of Brand Street, where the football supporters' coaches parked. We were there to sell the Saturday lunchtime papers, the *Evening Times* and the *Evening Citizen*. We would sell a lot more of the *Citizen* because it came with a pullout, a double-page-sized poster.

The buyer was given the choice of a Rangers or Celtic poster. So we quickly learned to say come on the Gers, or come on the Tic, whichever got you the bigger tip. The great thing about selling the papers was that most people gave you ten pence and told you to keep the change. The paper was only six pence, so there was plenty of cash to be made.

The papers sold it would be back to Cessnock Street to watch cars. On match days Charlie and I covered one side of the street, Searcher and Bobby the other. This time Searcher had an extra helper, because he had been landed with looking after his younger brother, Colin, who was only six. He was a pain in the arse, always whingeing and threatening to grass Searcher to his ma or da for even minor transgressions.

Then we would go along to Ibrox Park and collect empty bottles. Irn Bru bottles got you a penny and empty wine bottles got you a ha'penny. It doesn't sound much but between the five of us we could collect hundreds of bottles during the game. Then as soon as we saw the crowds start to leave the stadium it was a sprint back to Cessnock

Street to gather cash from the punters who hadn't paid up front for us to 'watch' their cars.

It was going to be a wonderful day.

At eleven the supporters' buses started to arrive. Charlie and I were allocated the Rangers end of the street. Searcher and Bobby took the Celtic end, along with Colin, who was already whingeing about having to walk the extra two hundred yards to where the Celtic buses were parked.

I had never seen anything like it. There were thousands of people getting off hundreds of huge coaches. They all headed in one direction, a tidal wave of giants. As the day was cold there was a cloud of steam above the heads of the fans, coming from their breath. Jostling among this sea of humanity were a few children, trying to keep up with their fathers. Searcher had to keep tugging at Colin's collar to stop him getting lost in the crowd.

This was not a day for children. It was a man's world. The aggression in the air was tangible. Bursts of song would break out in different parts of the crowd and, on occasion, they would all join in for a few lines. When they did, it was usually at the most bitter parts of the chants: 'Up to our knees in Fenian blood' or 'Fuck the Queen'.

It was not the carnival atmosphere I had expected, but it was exciting. All that raw emotion got your heart pumping and it was impossible not to join in with the chants.

I realise now there is a drum-thumping rhythm to most of these party songs. They appeal to a basic animal instinct, encouraging us to follow the herd. I joined in because it was exciting to be part of something so big. When I eventually stopped drinking in the atmosphere, and ceased to be astounded by the sheer number of people, I knuckled down to the job of selling newspapers.

Business was brisk. To replenish our stock there was a van on the middle of Brand Street that we had continually to run back to. We were given the papers a quire – a bundle of twenty-five – at a time. Around each bundle there was a paper strap. These straps of paper were very important, because they determined your wages. We were paid ten pence per quire and that day I earned £2.20. Charlie earned £1.90. We had sold almost a thousand newspapers between us. Incredible.

As soon as we had run out of papers, it was time to move on to our next money-making scheme: collecting empty bottles. Bobby and Searcher arrived with two beat-up old prams, which were kept in Searcher's close for occasions like this. Colin was sitting in one, like an oversized toddler. Charlie and I were delegated the Paisley Road side of the stadium while Searcher, Bobby and Colin took Govan Road.

The money we made selling newspapers we got to keep, but whatever we made from collecting empty bottles would be split five ways. This was to prevent squabbling or even fistfights over a wine bottle that was worth a ha'penny. The most common and long-running dispute was always who the bottle belonged to. Was it the person who spotted it or the person who picked it up? So we agreed to share the spoils.

That afternoon we filled both prams more than twice over, and made £3.60 between us. There was a minor dispute when I accused Searcher of lying about the amount of money he had got for the first pram-load. I insisted he must have been paid at least double what he told us. It was resolved when Charlie whispered in my ear that he had only handed over half of the money he had received for our first load.

It was now after half-four and almost completely dark. We were outside the stadium debating whether we should all head back to Cessnock or whether two of us should wait and try to get into the stadium at full time. There were many more empty bottles inside than outside. A decision was made that Searcher and Charlie would stay and quickly collect bottles inside the stadium and that Bobby and I would take Colin with us and race back to Cessnock for the car-watching money.

As Bobby and I were leaving, a side gate opened and Searcher and Charlie made a beeline for it. They managed to convince the steward to let them in. Colin ran across to his brother and, using his real name, said, 'Billy, let me come in as well. I've never been inside. Please, or I'm telling my ma you sent me with your pals instead of watching me.'

Searcher was torn. He wanted rid of Colin but could see the grief he would get if he fobbed him off to us and was then grassed up. 'Right okay, but you better stay beside me. Don't move from my side. It's heaving in here.' The steward tousled Colin's hair as he closed the gate behind them.

'Fuck off son. Not today okay. Just go home to your mammy and get a cuddle,' one of the car owners told me. He was the third person to say that, or something like it, in the last five minutes.

Rangers must have got hammered. Their fans were in a foul mood. One guy said to me: 'How can you stand there begging? Have you no shame?'

I was bewildered. You often got miserable people who would give you either a slap round the ear or the rough side of their tongue rather than part with a copper. But this was different. One elderly man shook his head and waved a go-away gesture at me as he got into his car. He was crying. This bewildered me even more.

What had the score been to provoke such a reaction?

Bobby came across. 'We better stop this Danny. That big guy over there with the black coat just told me that something really bad happened at the football and that we should piss off and stop annoying people.'

Now I began to understand why everyone was in such a foul mood. We made for home. As we walked across to the entrance of my close I heard my name being shouted. 'Danny, Danny. Come here.' It was my da and Donnie returning from the match. They were rushing towards us.

'What was the score?' I asked.

My da hugged me. 'I don't have a clue son. Where's Charlie?'

'Along at Ibrox, collecting more ginger bottles,' I told him, puzzled that he didn't know the score when he had just got back from the ground.

Da's grip tightened. 'Where, where at Ibrox? What do you mean at Ibrox? Is he in the fuckin' stadium? Where do you mean?' He was almost hysterical. His face was white. He looked terrified.

I burst out crying and sobbed, 'I don't know Da. A steward let him and Searcher inside the ground with about five minutes to go. But that was nearly an hour ago. He must still be collecting bottles.'

My da looked at Donnie, who had tears in his eyes. My brother shrugged. 'He could be anywhere Da. There must be fifty thousand people wandering about. All we can do is go back and see if we can find him.'

I was still crying. A panic had set in. 'Why Da? What's the matter Da? What's happened to Charlie, Da?'

'I don't know son. I don't know.' But the look in his eye betrayed him. He thought he might know. Whatever it was terrified him.

Donnie and my da hurried away. I rushed after them. 'Wait for me Da. I'm coming with you.'

'No Danny. You go up and tell your ma not to worry. We'll find Charlie. Go on. Be a good boy. Go up and tell your ma.'

I wailed through my tears, 'Tell her what Da? I don't get it. Tell her what?'

Donnie looked across at my da with a questioning look and when he nodded Donnie leaned down and looked me in the eye. 'There's been a terrible accident at Ibrox. I think a wall collapsed. There's a load of ambulances along there and . . . .' his voice breaking before he continued '. . . and we seen them carrying a lot of people out who had . . . .' again hesitating, and looking at my da, before continuing '. . . been killed. It looked like hundreds of them Danny. It looked like hundreds.'

I screamed: 'I canny tell her that. Don't make me tell her that. Please Da. I can help you look. Please Da.' I was sobbing as I held on to his arm.

Tears were streaming down his face. 'Come on, move it. Show me where you last seen him,' he said, dragging me along as his pace quickened. 'Come on.'

We couldn't get within a hundred yards of the stadium. The police had formed a thin blue line and no one was allowed any closer. We could hear them saying, 'Stay where you are sir. Please let the ambulance boys do their job.'

There was anger in their voices. Anger at the people who wanted to stare, the ones who wanted a story to tell the next day, the ones who wanted to say, 'I was there and I saw it all.'

Donnie pulled on my da's arm: 'Look Da. There's Archie Brown.' He was the policeman who had been at our house on Christmas Eve.

They both went towards him. 'Archie, Archie,' my da called out.

But Brown was busy telling a boy of about sixteen, 'If I need to move you again son, you're going to be sorry. Now fuck off before I put my boot up your shiter.'

'Archie, Archie,' my da tried again. This time he was heard.

Brown turned and faced Da. 'Davie, Donnie. What the hell are you doing here? You're not the type to be sniffing around something like this.'

My da said, 'Charlie's missing. He was in the stadium with Searcher and his wee brother. Have you seen any of them?'

The cop was shocked. 'No Davie, I haven't. But there's hundreds of weans all over the place. I wouldn't know if I had seen them even if I had.' Brown realised this wasn't an adequate response so he took my da aside and said quietly, possibly so I couldn't hear.

But I did.

'Davie you need to go to the main entrance. They have set up a . . . .' He hesitated: 'They have set up a temporary morgue. If you tell them you can't find your boy, they will take a description from you and go and check. I'm sorry Davie. I can't go with you. I need to stay here and try to keep the fuckin' vultures back.' As he spoke the last few words he raised his voice so that the 16-year-old boy he had been shouting at would hear and take the hint. He didn't.

'Take him home,' my da said to Donnie, pointing at me.

I screamed again. 'No, I'm staying with you Da. I'm staying with you Da.'

He looked again at Donnie. 'Take him home,' his tone of voice making clear it wasn't a matter for debate. Even in my terrified state, I could see that.

Donnie had to drag me along the street. I was distraught. This was my fault. How could I be so greedy? We had made plenty of money. How could I have sent him back in to try for more?

I hadn't, of course. But that didn't matter. Whatever had happened to Charlie had been my fault. He was my responsibility. He was my little brother.

As we neared the house, Darlene came rushing out of the close. 'Where have you lot been? My ma's going mental. It's on the news. Loads of people have been killed at the football. Where's my da?'

'Calm down Darlene. My da's along at Ibrox. Charlie's gone missing,' Donnie said.

Darlene was incredulous. 'Charlie's sitting at the kitchen table, with Bobby, counting the money they made.'

I don't know whether Donnie was holding me up, or I was holding him, but we sunk to our knees with relief. Darlene looked at us as if we were daft.

Donald and Dunky were despatched to fetch my da and let him know everyone was safe and well. When I went upstairs and my ma grabbed me for a hug she looked much older than her years. I was sobbing inconsolably as she held me close. I'm not sure why she was so sad. Everyone was okay.

I should have been happy, or, if not happy, then angry at Charlie for once again putting me through the mill. I was neither. I think it was sobs of relief. I couldn't bear to consider what would have happened had Charlie not been all right.

It took over an hour for my da and my two oldest brothers to get back from Ibrox. Dot speculated there would be a visit to one of the pubs between Ibrox and home, although my da denied this when he turned up. While the smell on his breath made him a liar, on this occasion no one could blame him.

About three hours later Darlene called out from the living room, 'Ma, come and see this.' She was standing by the window, pointing down at a police car that had pulled up across the road, directly in front of the close where Searcher lived.

My ma's hands went to her face. 'Oh my god. Not Searcher. Not that poor wee soul. Oh god, he's only ages with you Danny. Oh dear god, not him,' she sobbed.

It wasn't. Two police officers got out of the front. One of them opened the back door and let Searcher out. His head was down, so I couldn't work out whether he was in trouble or not. But the police-man closest to him was being gentle. His arm was round Searcher's shoulder.

'Oh thank god, thank god,' my ma said, crossing herself.

As the close door shut behind Searcher and the two policemen, Charlie squeezed in between us at the window. 'Where's wee Colin?' he asked.

Colin's funeral took place three days later. He was one of sixty-six people who died that day.

It wasn't a wall that collapsed at Ibrox; it was a metal barrier.

When Charlie, Searcher and Colin had gone into the stadium, Charlie became separated from them almost immediately. So he had looked for them for fifteen minutes, got fed up and come home along the Govan Road, knowing nothing of the frantic activity at the Paisley Road side of the stadium. He was as oblivious as the thousands of supporters who left via the Govan end, many of whom knew nothing of the disaster until reading the newspapers the following day.

Hundreds of people turned out for Colin's funeral. Cessnock Street was black. Women wept openly. It could have been their child. Local children were drawn to Ibrox, to the roars of the crowd, to the income to be made from watching cars, selling papers and collecting empty bottles.

It could have been any one of us.

17

The rest of that winter was bleak. I don't just mean the weather. There was a lingering sadness about, with fewer children playing on the streets. We would normally have fifteen-a-side street football matches every other night: Cessnock Street versus Middleton Street or games of kick the can with thirty boys and girls. All that stopped.

The children who were out were huddled at close entrances or in the bus shelter on Paisley Road. Everything was darker. We had hardly seen Searcher. Whenever we called for him his ma would find something he had to do for her or his da would be just about to take him somewhere.

Searcher had more brothers and sisters than me but Colin was the youngest, the baby. Searcher was back to being the baby now. The funny thing was he didn't protest much. If my ma told either me or Charlie we couldn't go out, we would raise merry hell. But Searcher would say 'Okay Ma', turn to us and shrug his shoulders with a what-can-you-do-look on his face.

For a while Charlie stopped coming with me when I was trying to coax Searcher out of the house. He became uncomfortable with the attention from Searcher's ma. When he was close, she would hug him and kiss the top of his head while smelling his hair. He would wriggle until she let him go, a look of hurt on his face. It was hurt at being embarrassed by an adult and not able to do anything about it. When Charlie mentioned this excessive cuddling to my ma, she had done exactly the same thing: hugged him tight, smelled his hair and kissed his head. Strange or what?

Gradually, our gang was complete again. Searcher was a bit quieter but still willing and able to sniff out trouble, especially if there was the possibility of making money. A car wash, he said one day. That's what Cessnock Street needed. An assembly-line car wash, just like the professional one along under the Kingston bridge. It had premises and forty staff, but the four of us could do the same thing on a Sunday morning.

In fact, we could do better. We could go to the customer instead of the customer coming to us. All we needed was a couple of buckets, a few sponges and a bottle of Squeezy washing-up liquid.

Charlie wasn't happy. 'Stick the sponge and the bucket up your arse Searcher. The water's freezing and the sponge has got holes all over it. I'm not cleaning this big van for ten pence. Stick the bucket and sponge right up your arse,' he insisted, standing back, arms folded.

'Sponges are supposed to have holes in them you halfwit,' I pointed out.

'Aye, but not holes that you can put your hand through,' my little brother retorted, demonstrating by pulling the sponge up to his elbow, like an inflatable armband.

'You get used to the water being cold after a while,' Bobby said.

'That's because your hands go numb. Just like your brain, you dimwit,' Charlie responded.

Searcher laughed and I said to Charlie, 'And anyway it's thirty pence. Not ten pence.'

Charlie looked at Searcher, who laughed again. 'Ten pence is Charlie's cut. The rest goes into the company pot.'

I wasn't having it. 'This company pot. Is that the same as your pocket? Because me and you are going to fall out if it is.'

'No, no,' he says. 'What happens is this. We, me and you, go round the doors and drum up customers. Twenty pence for a car wash and thirty pence for a van. The twenty pence is split: five pence for whoever gets the customer; ten pence for whoever washes the car; five pence in the company pot for new sponges and buckets or to give old Mrs McLeod a box of Quality Street for letting us fill up our buckets. If it's thirty pence for a van then the seller gets ten pence, the washer gets ten pence and ten pence goes into the pot. That's fair, isn't it?'

Charlie chipped in: 'You can stick your bucket and sponge up your arse. I'm offski. This is shite.' He dropped the bucket, threw down the sponge – what was left of it – at Searcher's feet and left.

'Will I finish the van off Search?' Bobby asked.

I was fifty-fifty. Should I follow Charlie and resign? Or was ten pence a van better than a kick in the balls?

'No, we split everything three ways and if we need to buy new sponges or anything else we chip in for it. Fuck this company-pot shite,' was my very reasonable proposal.

Searcher struggled with reasonable. If there wasn't something in it for him he didn't get involved. 'Okay,' he conceded, 'we split it three ways, but I'll look after yours Bobby and we can divi up at the end of the day. Okay?'

'Okay Search, whatever you say. You're the boss,' Bobby smiled.

'It must be fantastic having a big pet you don't need to feed,' I said. Searcher laughed, while Bobby looked puzzled.

While we were grafting, Charlie sat at our living-room window with what looked like a cup of tea and a pile of rich-tea biscuits. He watched us all day, whether we were washing cars, coming out of Mrs McLeod's close with an overflowing bucket of freezing-cold water or running across to the corner shop for another bottle of Squeezy.

'How much?' Charlie asked, as soon as I came into the house, my work done for the day. I ignored him and went straight to the bedroom, pulling my soaking-wet trousers, Y-fronts and socks off as I moved.

'How much?' he asked again. He was standing, eating a piece and jam, the jam being more around his mouth than in it.

'Mind your own business, shitebag,' I answered, struggling to remove the wet vest that had stuck to my back.

'Less than a pound then,' he sniped.

'How do you work that out?' I asked, knowing that I had eighty pence in my pocket. Not much for four hours work with ice-cold water. And I wouldn't have been surprised if I had contracted pneumonia.

'Because I can count,' he said, his reply muffled by another big bite of his piece, which left another smear of jam on his cheek.

'Do you want to count how many times I can punch you in the head?' I asked casually.

'If you like,' he replied, in the same tone. 'And then I can count how many times I can kick you in the balls?'

It was Dot who waddled out and separated us a few minutes later.

'For god's sake, you two. Does everything have to be a fight? Why can you two not just play nice once in a while? Danny, go and put pants on. You're too old to be showing your wee man.'

I turned scarlet and bolted into the bedroom.

Charlie laughed. 'Danny's a flasher, Danny's a pervert.' He turned to Dot. 'And anyway we were playing nice. He's still breathing isn't he?'

18

As I got dressed I heard the front door open and Annie shouting, 'Hello it's me. Who's in? Dot? Maggie?'

Dot called back, 'We're in the kitchen Annie. Danny, come and make a pot of tea.' Then, after hesitating, 'But make sure you put your wee man away first,' she cackled.

Annie looked into my bedroom as she passed. 'I wish I had said that to your brother, son,' cradling her pregnant belly and joining in the cackling.

More tea. No wonder they were always threatening to piss themselves. All they did was drink tea, which, as usual, I had to make.

My ma put down her *Sunday Post*: 'Is it May the eighteenth for you Annie?' as Annie tried manoeuvring her belly into place as she sat at the table.

'Christ, it's tight in this kitchen Maggie. There's hardly room to sit at this table now,' Annie said, puffing and panting. My ma smiled.

'No, it's the eighteenth for me Ma, the twenty-second for Annie and the twenty-eighth for you,' Dot clarified. She also pulled a chair out and squeezed her belly in against the table.

'All of us less than eight weeks then,' my ma said, as Darlene bounced into the room.

'Eight weeks to what?' she asked, opening the fridge door and sticking her head inside. 'I'm starving Ma.'

'Eight weeks till we have our weans, eejit. And how can you be starving? You're just after eating three pieces and jam?' Dot observed, getting annoyed.

'You eat like a pig at the best of times and you're still a skinny wee runt,' Annie joined in.

'Youse are just jealous because youse canny see your toes without a mirror,' Darlene retorted, peeling a triangle of Dairylea cheese and popping it in her mouth whole.

'Don't eat all the cheese young lady. That's for your da's pieces tomorrow,' my ma instructed.

Darlene was, as always, petulant. 'There's never anything to eat in this bloody house. If it's not them two scoffing everything in sight,' she said, pointing at Annie and Dot, 'then it's the three boys.'

I didn't rise to the bait. I was keeping my mouth shut. Making the tea and listening. I didn't know yet what hormones were, and what monsters they created. But I did know that for the past couple of months the most innocuous remark in this kitchen was liable to result in a tantrum. The safest thing to do was to speak only when spoken to and even then in very short sentences.

'See if I could get up Darlene, I would knock you into the middle of next week,' Dot said. 'It's not as if you put anything into that fridge. You swan about with your arse cheeks hanging out the bottom of thae hot pants. Are you gonny ever take them off by the way? You act like Lady Muck. Well you wait hen. Because someday you'll be bloody pregnant and we can all have a laugh at your fat arse.'

Donnie stepped into the kitchen, opened the fridge and stuck his head inside: 'Don't listen to them Darlene. At least when you're pregnant you'll get boobs to go with your fat arse, instead of being as flat-chested as a boy.'

'Donnie, leave her alone. She's just turned fourteen. It's too soon for all that,' Annie said.

That didn't stop me and Donnie from sniggering.

'Ma, gonny tell them,' Darlene screeched and huffed out of the room, arms folded across her nonexistent chest.

'That's not nice Donnie. Stop teasing her. She's worried about that you know. All her wee pals are developing faster. So don't do it again. You're just encouraging the younger boys to do the same,' Annie said, gesturing at me before continuing. 'Anyway now that you're here and not sitting on your arse in front of that telly, maybe you can come and talk to me about the wedding. The minister wants us to turn up at church on a Sunday. He's not happy about us getting married in a church we don't go to.'

'Fine. Tell him to stick his church. We'll get married in Martha Street registry office,' Donnie replied.

'Is my da away down the Rolls Royce club for a game of snooker Ma?' Donnie asked, walking out of the kitchen without waiting for an answer. It was a rhetorical question. It was Sunday afternoon. Where else would my da be?

Annie was on his case. 'Donnie, don't walk away. There are things we need to get sorted.' But the front door closed before she had finished her plea.

'Bloody useless article. Worse than his da at times,' my ma said.

'He's not any worse than Tony but,' Dot moaned. 'He told me that I've to stop asking him about the wedding. He's gave me every penny he's got and he's been and got measured for a hire suit and that's it. He will do his best to turn up sober and say whatever it is he needs to say, but other than that it's down to me. Then he started to walk out the door, just like Donnie just done.'

Dot took a breath and continued. Nobody tried to interrupt. 'So I say to him: "Do you not even want to know where we are having the reception?"

'"No!" he says.

"Well okay then," I say. "It's in the Masonic halls on Butterbiggins Road."

'That put his gas at a peep. He comes storming back in: "Don't be so stupid," he says, "none of my family will go to a Masonic hall. We're getting married in the chapel you eejit. How can we go from the chapel to the Orange lodge? Are you mental, woman?"'

"It's not the Orange lodge. It's the Masonic halls," I say to him.'

'And he says, "It's the same difference. We canny have the wedding in some Hun shop."'

'And just then my da walked in and that was them two into it as well. I'm booking the Masonic halls and if his family don't come then to hell with them. I don't care,' Dot concluded, out of breath.

Annie giggled and my ma laughed. 'Do you feel better with that off your chest hen?' As she said it, Darlene came back into the kitchen. She had heard the end of the row and wailed: 'Now youse are even talking about my chest. It's not fair.' Then she stormed out again.

My ma shook her head while Annie giggled again. 'It's just as well we weren't talking about them wee birds you get. What are they called again? Oh aye, blue tits.' They laughed uproariously, but I noticed they had their legs crossed as well.

Dot got over her laughing. 'Just ignore her Ma. She'll get over it. Anyway what will we do? Me and Annie went up and put a deposit down at the Masonic hall. I never thought for a minute his family would have a problem with that. If there was a cheaper Catholic hall somewhere I would have booked it. Do you think his family will come?'

'I don't know Dorothy. His ma is a bitter wee soul. I'm a Catholic myself but that doesn't mean I hate Protestants. Just as well really, what with all my weans being wee Proddies. You will need to ask them. Go and see his ma and da and tell them you've booked the Masonic halls. If that isn't to their liking all they have to do is give you back the money for the deposit and you can find somewhere else. But four weeks isn't a long time to find another hall.'

'Oh Christ. Why have I got myself involved with such a useless article? You would think he would do some of the running about for me,' Dot sighed.

'Och he's not useless hen. Well not any more useless than most men. At least he's working. That's more than you can say for some,' Annie piped up. 'Not all men are useless. Put the kettle on again for the tea, Danny.'

She raised her cup, pointed it at me and grinned.

19

'We've only got a week Tony. Don't be so bloody useless, and stop irritating me. As if this effing wean of yours isn't irritating me enough. Piles it's gave me now. Bloody piles. I'm seventeen years old. I feel like seventeen stone and I've got piles that I can't even reach to scratch. Now, with a week to go to our wedding, you tell me that the house we are supposed to be moving into is getting demolished. Why are you such a useless bastard Tony?' Dot groaned, struggling to get to her feet from the living-room sofa.

'And come here and help me up instead of standing there looking glaikit. Hurry up. I need a pee, *again*,' she screamed.

She wobbled to the bathroom with a strange side-to-side gait. To be fair, my sister was big. At first my granny reckoned it could have been twins but then decided she was probably full of water – Dot I mean, not my granny.

'What happened, Tony? I thought your da said you definitely had that house at the end of McLean Street. It was in an awful state but at least it was a house,' my ma asked. She also struggled to her feet and waddled over to the window. I don't know why, but it seemed to me that if my ma didn't look out of the window every five minutes she would burst.

'It was supposed to be ours Maggie, but then some high heid yin at the council decided that the whole of McLean Street was to be demolished, along with Blackburn Street. They are going to build a load of new houses all over Kinning Park. It's not my fault is it? I don't know how that makes me a useless bastard. I really don't,' he said, feeling sorry for himself. Something I could understand.

Dot, never easy to get on with, had turned into a monster over the last month. All she ever did was bite the head off Tony. Don't get me wrong, he was generally useless but, to be fair, not everything could be his fault. I mean, I heard her ripping him to shreds one night because the chippy had run out of fritters. Poor sod.

'Well I suppose that means you both have to stay here after the wedding then,' my da interjected, obviously not happy about the possibility.

'I think so Davie. I know it's not ideal. But it will only be for a wee while. Something will turn up,' Tony said, shrugging his shoulders and looking glaikit.

'Will it but Tony? Houses don't just turn up son. It's not like waiting for a taxi outside the pub. Houses don't just turn up. You need to extract your finger from your arse son and find something. "Not ideal," he says, "not ideal."'

'You can hardly swing a cat in here as it is son. Annie's already moved in with Donald, so they need their own room, Darlene's been papped on to the couch in the living room so they have a room to themselves. So if you move in where do we put the three boys? In the kitchen or the bathroom? Do you see what I mean son? You canny really wait for "something to turn up,"' my da said, laying on the heavy sarcasm at the end.

Dot returned from her long trek to the bathroom. Well it must have been a long trek considering how red her face was. She shouted at my da, 'Why don't you leave him alone? It's not his bloody fault. Why is everybody always blaming him for everything? That's my man Da. Stop bloody picking on him. You're not perfect either you know.'

Looking at my da's face made clear to me the meaning of 'flabber-gasted'. I was never that sure before. But his expression said it all. He was looking from side to side, trying to find someone to explain how Dot spent every waking minute criticising Tony but when he gently said 'get your finger out son,' she was on him like a Rottweiler.

Dot wasn't finished. 'And by the way Da. Don't just stand there with your mouth open. I think I'm in bloody labour.'

'No, you canny be. You're not due for four weeks hen. Is it no' just wind?' he replied.

Years later I saw a film called *The Exorcist*, in which there was a young lassie who was possessed by the devil. In one scene she swivelled her head round with a look of pure evil on her face and spat vomit at a priest. Dot had that same look.

'No! It's not fucking wind. Get me to a hospital. This wean wants to come out.'

'Okay hen, calm down. I'll get Willie next door to give us a run to the Southern General in his van.'

Dot was sobbing. 'Da, Willie's got a fish van. Please, please, please. Just get an ambulance. Da, this is sore.'

Up to this point my da had seven children and another one on the way. This should have been a walk in the park, but, according to my ma, he had been drunk for the birth of every single one of us. Except for Charlie; when he was born my da was working away from Glasgow.

'Ooh, ah, oh, ah,' this came from my ma, who was sitting in the armchair nearest the fire.

'Oh shit, not you as well,' said my da. 'You canny both go into labour at the same time, for Christ's sake. Don't do that to me Maggie.'

My ma giggled. 'No, I'm sitting too near the fire. My ankles have went all tartan and got really itchy and I canny reach them for a scratch. Ooh ah. Danny, bring me one of thae knitting needles out of the sideboard drawer son. Hurry up will you?'

'Why the hell is that fire on anyway? It's nearly summer. Do youse lot think I'm made of money?' my da complained.

'Da, are you going to get me a bloody ambulance, or should I start walking to the Southern? I'll pay the electricity bill if you get me an ambulance right now. Please Da,' Dot pleaded, now doubled over in agony.

Darlene came into the room at her usual hundred miles an hour. 'I phoned an ambulance from Mrs Wilson's in the next close. The woman says it will be here within fifteen minutes,' she said breathlessly, putting her arms round Dot before adding, 'You'll be okay Dot. I'll come with you.'

Dot held her arm tightly and nodded. She continued breathing heavily as if she too had just run up the stairs.

'Does anybody want a cup of tea and some toast and jam?' was my contribution.

20

Except for New Year, I don't remember being up this late. The ambulance had come and taken Dot and Darlene away at about ten o'clock. Tony refused to go. He said this was women's stuff. They could wake him in the morning and tell him if it was a boy or a lassie.

It was now half-two in the morning. My da was sleeping in the armchair next to the fire but, funnily enough, no longer moaning about the fire being on. My ma hadn't moved from the window since Dot and Darlene left. She had had every intention of going with them but the ambulance men advised against it. Not good for the blood pressure, they said. But standing at the window for over four hours couldn't have been helping much.

Charlie was curled up asleep at my da's feet. He had insisted that if I was allowed to stay up then so should he be. My ma explained they were only letting me stay up to make her tea, but then relented and said he could stay up as well if he wanted. It was Friday night so there was no school the next day. He then promptly fell asleep in front of the fire ten minutes later.

'What was that?' my ma asked, moving from one end of the bay window to another.

'It sounds like a taxi,' I said.

'It is, Danny. Look. It's stopped at our close. Is that Darlene getting out?'

'Aye it is Ma. And look who's behind her – Dot.'

It took them a good five minutes to get up the stairs. By this time my da had been woken up by my ma and me, speculating as to why Dot was coming home, puffing and panting, rather than in a hospital bed.

Tony appeared in the living room, looking wide awake. 'I thought you were going to bed and we were to let you know in the morning what it was Tony,' I laughed.

'Aye well, I found it hard to sleep, you wee tube,' he smiled.

Dot waddled into the living room still tightly holding Darlene's arm. She looked at my da and he asked, 'Well?'

Dot collapsed onto the sofa. 'Wind. They gave me a packet of Rennies.'

My da shook his head and walked out of the living room, speechless.

Charlie stirred and let off a rip-roaring fart. 'You could have just done that,' he said, sleepily.

'Six days to go Danny,' Darlene said, as she grabbed my hands and tried to skip around me in the hallway.

'Get off me you halfwit,' I told her.

'I canny Danny. Oh that's like a wee poem isn't it? I canny Danny, I canny Danny. Hee hee. Auntie Wilma's coming the day with my bridesmaid's dress, Danny. It's beautiful. Wait till you see it. It's ivory and it's strapless and it's pure gorgeous. Wait till you see it Danny.'

Just before I managed to get out of her vice-like grip, Dunky stepped out of the bathroom, towelling his long hair dry. 'Oh look. Darlene and her wee sister Danielle are dancing about because their bridesmaid dresses are coming.'

Obviously, I went for him. But he put his hand on my head, keeping me at a distance, ensuring that my punches and kicks missed the target. 'He won't always be smaller than you Dunky. You better watch yourself in a few years,' Tony warned, emerging from the kitchen.

'Actually he better watch himself just now,' Charlie said as he came out from behind Tony. He ran at Dunky from behind and kicked him between the legs.

Dunky went down like a sack of totties, holding on to his bollocks with one hand and trying to push himself off the floor with the other hand. He was screaming, 'I'm going to kill you. You little bastard. I swear when I catch you, you're fucking deid.'

I walked past him and stood on the hand he was using to push himself up. 'You and whose army?' Charlie and I laughed and ran into the kitchen, looking for the relative protection of standing behind my ma's chair.

My ma, Dot and Annie were all in the kitchen, at the table. They were sitting sideways on because they couldn't reach their cups of tea if they sat facing the table like un-pregnant people.

Dunky came staggering into the kitchen: 'Both of you out here. Right now. I'll take the two of youse together.'

Dot said, 'Dunky, piss off and leave the weans alone. Why don't you grow up? Now piss off. By the way, don't go using my hairdryer again. You're going to knacker it.'

'And that goes for her mascara and rouge as well you poof,' Charlie said.

My ma slapped him across the back of the head. 'Mind your language you. Your brother's no' a poof.'

'No, that's not a nice word to use Charlie. You should say he's a homosexual,' I said, throwing a dish towel at Dunky.

Everybody laughed, except Dunky. He tried to get at us but we were on the other side of the kitchen table and between us were three heavily pregnant women. He had no chance.

'He's gonny batter you two and we won't always be in his way,' Annie said, in her most serious tone.

'He can try,' said Charlie. But I wasn't so flippant. Annie was right. Dunky could be a good laugh but kicking him in the bollocks was going too far. We would pay for it sooner rather than later.

My ma had sat unperturbed through our carry on. She must have been getting used to it. 'Don't you two go anywhere. Your auntie Wilma will be here in a wee while.'

I was behind her, putting the kettle on as usual, and asked, in my whiniest voice: 'Why? We seen her last week. We were going out to play football. Why do we need to stay in?'

'Because,' Dot said.

'Because what?' I asked.

'Just because,' Dot said emphatically.

'Well I'm no' staying in because of just because. That doesn't make sense, just because. What's that supposed to mean?'

'It means if you don't stay in I'm going to rattle your arse with the back of my hand Danny boy,' said Annie, grabbing me round the waist and trying to tickle me.

'She's bringing you two a wee surprise,' my ma smiled.

Charlie's eyes lit up. 'Is she? What is it? Is it good?'

I didn't like the sound of 'wee surprise'. Especially the way my ma looked at Annie and Dot, with the two of them putting their heads down and suppressing a laugh.

Auntie Wilma had arrived and while she was having her first cup of tea she asked how everybody was. She got some tales about piles and sore backs and shows, whatever that was. She then told us stories about her family, and how they were, before getting Darlene to try on her bridesmaid's dress. Everybody oohed and aahed.

'I might have to take it in a tiny wee bit around the bust and maybe even put some straps on it hen. We don't want it slipping down to your waist. After all, you're not overly well endowed are you hen? You poor soul,' Aunt Wilma sympathised.

Darlene's face fell. She had been so happy with the dress. Aunt Wilma was quick to reassure her: 'Don't be daft hen. You've got the look that the women on the telly and in all thae fashion shows want. You could be a model so you could. God knows I wish these were half the size. All they do is get in the bloody way,' she said, lifting her not inconsiderable bosoms with both hands.

Charlie and I collapsed into giggles but Darlene's face was transformed. She had at last discovered something positive aspect about being flat-chested. Aunt Wilma said she could be a model and Aunt Wilma was in the fashion industry – she worked in Shapiro's dress shop doing alterations. My sister was ecstatic. She pranced up and down the hall in that dress like Doris Day or Debbie Reynolds.

'And now boys, look what I've got for you,' Aunt Wilma said. She opened the zip front on a suit-carrier. All I could see was purple – a lot of purple and some cream-coloured lace.

'No way, not a chance. You must be joking,' I protested, moving quickly towards the door. 'That better not be for me.'

Aunt Wilma now had the thing completely out of the garment bag. It was a pageboy suit, in deep purple, with cream-coloured lace round the collars and cuffs of the jacket. The trousers – which Darlene held out to show us – were like pantaloons. There was also a pink shirt and an embroidered cream waistcoat.

'I like it,' was Charlie's reaction.

I turned bright red. I could hardly speak. 'You, you, you what? Are you crazy? You're going to look like Little Lord Fancy Boy. Are you kidding? No way man. Not me. I'm not wearing that. No chance. Never, never, never.'

I read somewhere years later that *never* is a word god invented so that every time he heard it he could have a laugh. Twenty minutes later, and with fifty pence in our pockets, we were standing on the kitchen table wearing the entire outfit, while Aunt Wilma tugged at our sleeves and collars.

My ma stood back and, with tears in her eyes, said, 'I can't believe how handsome you two are. Look at youse.' She turned to Dot, Annie and Darlene, who were also appreciative of our new look.

Dunky spoiled it when he came into the kitchen, eating a packet of crisps, pointing at us and laughing so hard that he was choking and spitting crisps and snotters everywhere. My ma pushed him out of the door but the damage was done. Charlie and I simultaneously took the jackets off and threw them onto the floor. The waistcoats and shirts followed and, finally, the pantaloons. It could have been choreographed. We jumped off the table in our underpants and socks and bolted.

We never saw those pageboy outfits again. Thank you, god.

21

The next few days went really quickly. There were literally hundreds of people in and out of the house. I don't think the Second World War took as much organising as this double wedding. Tony's family had eventually accepted the Masonic hall as a suitable venue. It was all down to money: when they were asked to refund the deposit to Dot, amazingly, they changed their minds about its suitability.

Dot and Tony's wedding was to be in the morning at St Constantine's chapel in Govan, so we had to be there by ten-thirty at the latest. The ceremony would start at eleven o'clock sharp. Apparently, the old priest had refused to marry a couple who turned up late. Donnie and Annie's wedding would follow later that day, at two. So a way had to be found to get everybody from Govan to Kinning Park parish church. For their part, Annie's family didn't care where it was as long as the food was free and the drink was cheap, or vice versa.

'My brother is a corporation bus conductor,' Tony announces three days before the wedding.

'That's fantastic Tony. Maybe we can get him to go along the pews and give everybody a wee ticket out of his machine,' Donnie said, with a look of derision.

'No, I mean, he told me last night that one of the drivers could borrow a bus and do us a wee favour. It would only cost twenty quid.'

'Are they allowed to do that?' my ma asked. 'Borrow a bus, just like that.'

'Well, strictly speaking, not really,' says Tony 'but he thinks nobody will notice.'

'How the hell can nobody notice a double-decker green-and-orange bus? Are you joking or what Tony?' Donnie said, laughing scornfully.

'There's hunners of buses down that depot. They're not going to miss one. It's sorted. The driver's gonny go down at five in the morning when most of the buses are coming out. Nobody stands there and counts the buses. He'll have his uniform on. My brother will also be there, as if he's the conductor, and bob's your uncle. We get a bus for the day for twenty quid. Everyone's a winner.'

It sounded foolproof, didn't it?

The morning of the weddings was upon us. The house was bedlam. There was one bathroom but two brides and one mother of the bride, all standing in a queue at seven in the morning. I was up, making tea of course.

I don't know if I had ever heard my ma shouting so loudly: 'Donnie, open this bloody door and get out of that bathroom right bloody now, or so help me god I will do you a mischief.'

She meant it. The bathroom door opened and Donnie emerged in his grey Y-fronts, two odd socks and nothing else. There were a couple of spots of yellow something on his chin, which was either dried vomit or the remains of his chicken korma from last night. I've seen three dead bodies in my whole life, but Donnie looked worse than any of them.

Annie burst out crying. 'What are you doing here? It's bad luck to see me before the wedding.'

My da emerged from the bathroom behind Donnie, also in his 'Y' fronts and socks – a matching pair, hallelujah – but thankfully without the dried vomit/korma. He said, 'I wouldn't worry about it Annie doll. He can't see you. He's still too drunk. Even if he could see you he wouldn't remember.'

'He's supposed to be at Tony's house, getting ready to get married Da. For god's sake. And where is Tony?' Dot asked.

My da stood aside so that we could see into the bathroom. Tony was sprawled out in the bath, naked. To preserve his modesty there was only a face cloth, with a picture of a little yellow duck on it. Now Dot was wailing too.

'Oh for Christ's sake. You two get in that kitchen,' my ma said, pointing at Annie and Dot. 'Danny make them some hot tea and a wee slice of toast. Davie, you take these two pathetic excuses for men and do something with them. If you can't sober them up by eleven then go and find somebody else to marry these lassies. Because they're getting married the day, no matter what. Mark my words.'

Dot and Annie were sitting at the kitchen table sobbing and snottering into dish towels when Darlene flounced in, singing, 'I'm getting married in the morning.' She said, 'What's the matter with them two? They're always greeting. I'm never getting pregnant.'

There's that *never* word again.

Dot and Annie continued to sob, ignoring Darlene, who grabbed a piece of toast and announced, 'Okay then, I'll be first in the bathroom,' before skipping out.

By the time I had finished making tea and toast for all and sundry, my da, Tony and Donnie had disappeared. They had presumably gone to Tony's, since that's where they had taken the hired suits the day before, on their way out to the stag. Incidentally, this pre-wedding tradition had started at nine in the morning, when Tony put half a can of lager on his Kellogg's corn flakes.

By now a relative calm had descended. Darlene was dressed and in consequence was the first to get her hair done by Shirley Anne, Annie's wee cousin, who was in her second year at hairdressing college. They were all having their hair put up so at least there was no cutting involved.

I'm sorry to say, and I know it sounds terrible, but Shirley Anne had a skelly eye. How could anybody trust her with a pair of scissors? You would have to be mental. Dot and Annie had both managed to get their make up on, and, apart from slightly puffy eyes they seemed happy enough. They were sitting on hard-back kitchen chairs in their underskirts. Actually they were full-length underskirts, so what would you call them? Under-dresses? Anyway, they were sitting there in the living room, waiting their turn to get their hair put up, when Annie asked, 'Where's Irene?'

'Irene who?' my ma replied.

Annie shook her head. 'My Irene, my big sister Irene. My bridesmaid Irene. Where the hell is she?'

There was much shrugging of shoulders and 'I don't knows'.

At that point Charlie came into the living room, carrying a bowl of Sugar Puffs with the milk almost overflowing. 'Have you checked Dunky's bed? She might still be in there.'

My ma sprang from her chair. Well as much as a woman in her mid-forties, who is eight months pregnant, can spring from a chair. 'He's only fifteen. The dirty besom that she is. What age is she? Twenty-two? Get her out of that bed Annie. Right now, before I bloody get her.'

Ten minutes later Annie came back into the living room. Irene was behind her, red-faced and shuffling into the seat beside Annie, trying to avoid my ma's eyes. 'Good luck with that hen,' I thought.

'Do you know he's only fifteen?' my ma asked.

Irene shook her head. 'No,' she answered, in a whisper.

'Well he is,' my ma confirmed. 'I hope you used something,' she went on, glancing at me to see if I was listening. I was. 'You get and put the kettle on,' she said, 'and take him with you,' indicating Charlie. But I was finding this funny so I stood quietly outside the door and listened.

'What will you do if your man finds out?' I heard my ma say. Irene started to cry softly and I could barely hear her reply.

'I don't know Mrs McCallister. He'll batter me if he does. Ian doesn't need much of an excuse at the best of times.'

'Sorry hen, but you will probably deserve it. What are you thinking about? A 15-year-old boy for heaven's sake.'

There was anger in my ma's voice but sympathy as well. She knew Irene's husband by reputation. He was handy with his fists and not exactly the faithful type if the rumours were true. I wasn't finding it so funny now.

'I didn't know he was only fifteen. He said he was seventeen. He looks seventeen, especially with that long blonde hair of his,' she whimpered.

'Any man, given a chance, will lie to you to get you into bed. Surely you know that. You're not a daft wee lassie hen. And listen to you talking about his hair. He's fifteen. Are you stupid?' my ma said, her sympathy fading.

Annie interrupted, bristling: 'She's not stupid Maggie. Well maybe a bit stupid where men are concerned. But then we all are if we're honest.' She smiled at her sister: 'It will be all right. I'll tell Dunky to keep his mouth shut. You just keep yours shut as well and stay away from him in future.'

'And one more thing,' my ma said. 'If Ian does find out, for his sake hen, you make sure he doesn't lift a hand to my Dunky. You will both be sorry if he does.' This wasn't said vindictively. My ma was being honest.

22

'Ten fifty-two and twenty seconds,' I answered Dot. It was the twelfth time she had asked me the time inside ten minutes.

'Is that a Mickey Mouse watch you've got on?' she asked, smiling.

'No, it's a Timex. Is that a Mickey Mouse man you're marrying?' I smirked.

We were in the bridal car going round and round the block beside the chapel. Tony hadn't arrived yet. In the car there was Dot, my da and the three junior members of the family – Darlene, Charlie and me. The three of us were supposed to be jumping on the subway to Govan Cross with the rest of the family. But time got short and my ma told us to get in with Dot.

Getting a lift in a fancy car would normally have been a big deal. But it meant Charlie and I missed the scramble when we pulled away from the close. In accordance with tradition my da had opened the window and thrown a big handful of copper coins out to the large group of boys and girls that had assembled. Of course, Searcher and Bobby got the lion's share. My dad had tipped them the wink a couple of days before and told them where to stand. He was as good as his word. He practically tossed the coins into Searcher's hands.

Before we came down to the car, we had been standing in the hall, nervously waiting. Then my da turned up. He had been at Tony's house all morning, staying out of the way. He wasn't as daft as he acted.

Da walked through the front door and Dot, Annie, my ma and Darlene were standing in a row, twittering on. He was at his most charming. 'In the name of the wee man. Will you look at this? Have there ever been four such gorgeous women in the same place at the same time? Dorothy you look as pretty as a picture, sweetheart. And Annie, if I wasn't attached hen, I would ask you to marry me so I would.

Darlene, darling, you will be able to take your pick of any man. You are stunning, absolutely stunning hen. You look like a model.'

Finally, he turned to my ma. 'Maggie, anybody can see where thae lassies get their good looks. My god, you are a beautiful woman. Sometimes I don't know how lucky I am.'

There was a tear in everyone's eye, including my da's. I say everyone. Not in mine. I thought my da was still drunk.

'What time is it now?' Dorothy nudged me and nodded towards my wrist, as if I didn't know where my watch was.

'Never mind. There he is,' my da said.

'Why is his da pushing him along like that Da? Do you think he's changed his mind?' Darlene asked, apparently innocently, although the grin she put on for me and Charlie wasn't at all innocent.

'Stop annoying your sister. There's nobody pushing him along,' my da said. 'Well not much,' he added, with a grin.

In fact Tony was being pushed along by his da. Tony was remonstrating with him and at the same time trying to fasten his braces on to his suit trousers. He spotted us and, with a big cheesy grin on his face, waved.

Now Dot had her say. 'What am I doing? I'm marrying that halfwit in less than five minutes. Look at him. He can't even hold his bloody trousers up. My god, what am I letting myself in for?' The words were harsh but her voice wasn't. There was true love in there, somewhere. I didn't hear it at the time but I can hear it now, despite everything that's happened since.

Everything went fine at the chapel. Tony managed to hold his trousers up. Dorothy managed to look radiant. The priest managed to ignore Dorothy's bump and the fact she was getting married in white.

During the ceremony my ma was sitting with tears streaming down her face. I heard my da whisper, 'Don't think of it as losing a daughter. Think of it as gaining an idiot.'

She slapped him on the arm, but it made her smile. When we got outside, everyone was throwing confetti. I raced Charlie to the bridal car, intending to be first inside, when my da caught us by the collars.

'Bride and groom only, wee men. You two wait for the bus with me,' he instructed, pulling us close.

The plan was for Dot and Tony to go straight to the hall and hang about for a couple of hours. The rest of us would go to Donnie and Annie's wedding and we would meet them at the hall later. On paper, it was a good idea. What nobody considered was that Tony's family, including Tony, would be drinking before the rest of us got there for two whole hours.

We were standing waiting outside the chapel, about sixty of us, counting uncles, aunts, cousins and friends that we had offered a seat on the bus. That included my granny and granda, my da's parents. They looked grim; I think they expected a car to be laid on.

Having done her bridesmaid duty, Darlene now had to take baby Paul back from her pal, who had been looking after him for most of the morning. Or should I say when he wasn't getting passed around and admired in his wee sailor suit. Darlene would probably be stuck with him for most of the day. It must be terrible being a lassie, I thought.

My ma was worried. 'Davie, what will we do if Tony's brother doesn't turn up with the bus?'

'Kick his head in probably,' Dunky remarked.

'I don't think that will get us to Kinning Park in time for the wedding. Will it Duncan?' my ma answered sternly. Oh, oh, full name. Time to shut it Dunky.

My da looked daggers at Dunky and did his best to reassure my ma. 'Don't worry Maggie. It will be fine. He would have let us know if there was a problem. He wouldn't just leave us standing here with our thumbs up our ar . . . . In fact, there he is now.'

My da was exceptionally calm, I thought. Then I noticed he got calmer every time he took a sip from the flask in his jacket pocket.

'Thank god for that,' my ma said. 'I couldn't have walked to the subway. I need to sit down before I fall down. My feet are swelling up like balloons.'

The bus pulled up right in front of the chapel doors. Three people got off. When my da and I got on there were another fifteen or so people sitting on the bus. Tony's brother, Simon, was at the side of the bus, talking to the driver.

My da marched round and grabbed a hold of Simon. 'Hey Simple. What the fuck is this? You said we would have the bus to ourselves.'

'Aye well, Davie. It's like this big man. We drove out of the garage at five this morning as planned. But somebody had left the number turned to 54. So as we approached stops, people put their hands out. What could we do? We couldnae have people complaining that there was a number 54 just running right by them, could we? So we started picking them up and dropping them off. But it's fine, because I've changed the number to 52 now, and the 52 finishes at Kinning Park. So as soon as we get there, this lot will get off and we will change the sign to 'not in service'. Makes sense big man. Know what I mean like?'

'Aye I know exactly what you mean Simple. What you mean is you've been earning money since five o'clock this morning driving this bus about and taking full fares. That means you won't be looking for that twenty quid off my Donnie. That's what you mean isn't it Simon?' my da said, not unpleasantly.

Simon glanced at the driver, who nodded his agreement, and then came the concession. 'Exactamundo Davie. Got it in one. Everyone's a winner eh.'

Simon moved round to the side of the bus, where people were starting to get on. 'Come on people. Let's get on the jolly old wedding bus. Make sure you have the right change ready.' He looked at my ma: 'Joke, Mrs M. Just my wee joke,' putting one arm round her shoulders to help her up the first step.

My ma brushed past, almost knocking him over in the process. 'Chancer,' she mumbled. At least Simon had the good sense to look embarrassed.

Donnie was pacing up and down outside the church when we got there, nervously puffing at a roll-up. It must have been burning his fingers it was that short and skinny. Dunky – Donnie's best man – was standing at the door talking to Shirley Anne, the skelly-eyed hair-dresser. He must have been making progress because she was looking at him with an interested expression. When I say looking *at* him, she was actually looking over his shoulder, but you know what I mean.

My ma was first off the bus. She had sat right next to the door in case she needed to dash for a pee when we got there. She saw what Dunky was up to with Shirley Anne.

'Dunky, come here right now,' she shouted, before her feet touched the ground. She grabbed him by the ear, getting a handful of his hair at the same time, and pulled his head down to her mouth. 'Has that bloody thing down there not got you into enough bother? Will you never bloody learn boy? Get over beside your brothers, and the next time I see you talking to any more lassies the day I'll be cutting it off. Do you understand?'

As she let go of his ear, and his hair, he put his arm round her shoulder and pulled her close, kissing her on the cheek. 'Of course I understand Ma. By the way you look gorgeous, so you do.'

She smiled. Daddy's boy right enough.

Annie was fashionably late by ten minutes. The bride's prerogative they say. Donnie managed four more roll-ups in that ten minutes. So much for him not being bothered. This ceremony also went without a hitch although Donnie was, unusually, so soft spoken it was a struggle to hear him. Annie was beaming all the way though. She was the happiest person I had seen all day. She appeared not to have a care in the world.

We discovered later that evening that she had been in labour since one o'clock.

'Right that's that done then.' Donnie was standing on the church steps taking everyone's congratulations. 'Time for a drink wee man. What do you think?' he said, grabbing Charlie, lifting him in a bear hug and swinging him round.

'Make mine's a pint of heavy,' said Charlie. He wasn't joking.

23

As soon as we got to the hall Tony's da approached us, weaving all over the place: 'Whose idea was this? Fuckin' Masonic halls. Is this a fuckin' wind up or what?'

My da was still sober. 'Christopher, come in and take a wee half. The drink in here is dead cheap and I'm sure you won't be excommuni-cated for drinking Protestant whisky if it's as cheap as this. I'm also pretty sure I've seen that fat priest of yours filling his boots in here. Come on man,' he cajoled. Tony's da reluctantly accompanied him to the bar, although by the state of him, I don't think he had had a problem doing that on his own.

The hall was typical of that type of venue. At one end there was a stage, where the DJ was setting up his equipment. At the other end there was a bar, which was crowded as the guests had just arrived. There was a long row of tables across the front of the stage. This was where the wedding party would sit. The rest of the tables were randomly placed around the dance floor and guests were invited to please themselves where they sat. There was no formal seating plan. The hope was that the three families would mingle.

That hadn't happened. Tony's family had taken the tables nearest to the bar, and there was a multitude of brothers, sisters, aunties, cousins, uncles and grandparents. At least fifty. And that didn't include Tony's friends, which added another twenty to the total. Quite a crowd for one side to bring.

Meanwhile, Annie's family had taken up residence nearest the long tables against the far wall, which were heaving with buffet. That is if you could call plates piled high with sausage rolls and sandwiches and some paper bowls filled with trifle and a plastic spoon a proper buffet.

They weren't too bothered about being so far away from the bar, judging by what I saw. Most of them had brought their own booze, and they gave the game away by looking round surreptitiously before putting an empty glass under the table. These, miraculously, came up full, unless of course there were midget waitresses under the table.

My family was left with the tables in the middle of the hall. Not that any of the McCallisters were bothered. They were halfway between the bar and the buffet and practically on the dance floor. It didn't get any better. They could eat, drink and be merry. Happy days. At the top table the wedding party consisted of the two brides and their grooms, the parents of the brides and grooms and the two best men and two bridesmaids.

The first problem occurred when Tony's granny, on his mother's side, sat down beside him at the top table. I could see my ma and da glance at each other and then at Dot. She in turn was glaring at Tony, who was sitting beside her. He silently mouthed, 'What can I do?' and shrugged his shoulders.

Dot mouthed back, 'move her'. Tony looked at his new wife as if she had asked him to pick his granny up and kick her across the hall. He mouthed back, 'You fuckin' move her,' before getting to his feet and walking away.

Dunky did his best to ease the situation. 'Are you quite comfy there auld yin? Well you stay right where you are and I'll go and sit at the weans' table. You never know. I might get a wee grip of that blonde waitress behind the bar if I'm sat down there.'

Tony's granny showed real class with her reply: 'I should fuckin' think so. I am his only fuckin' granny you know.' She then emptied her vodka and coke in one swallow. My ma rolled her eyes at my da but he grinned and shrugged his shoulders.

The speeches went smoothly. Apart, that is, from Dunky asking Tony's granny if he could sit on her knee and give his speech because there was no place at the top table since she had taken his seat. This was said in a jovial way but her reaction was anything but: 'An auld pensioner canny even get a seat at her favourite grandson's wedding when she's practically on her last legs! What's the bloody world coming to, I ask you? It won't be that long before I meet my maker you know.' This was said as she swiftly emptied her third glass of free champagne.

Nobody was seriously offended by the speeches. However, I noticed Donnie looking daggers at Tony's mates, who were continuously talking over the speeches and being boisterous. He did his best to ignore their behaviour but, eventually, his patience ran out. 'If all the ex altar boys could calm down, I might get through this speech without embarrassing myself.' One or two of them stood up to reply but their pals pulled them back and did their best to calm things down.

The speech from Annie's Da's was a mumble from start to finish, less than thirty words long. But the tears on his face as he raised his glass to Annie told the real story I suppose.

My da's speech was the best. As usual he had the girls, including my ma, giggling and blushing, and the men nodding their heads in agreement. His last words, greeted by cheers and applause, were 'and let the games begin'. And begin they did.

I noticed the hall manager approaching my da and whispering something. My da shook his head, vehemently. I got a bit closer. This could be interesting.

'That's bloody ridiculous,' my ma said to my da. 'It's a wedding, for god's sake. How can they expect us to do that?'

I noticed the staff moving about ten tables from near the dance floor into the corner furthest away from the stage. To do this they had to rearrange some of my family; and some of Tony's family as well. There was an understandable grumbling because people were being crammed into tables where there was little space. Others who had been up dancing or at the toilet came back to find that their table, and drinks, had disappeared.

I noticed my da going round the tables explaining the situation. There had been a loss of electric power in the room next door, which was also a function suite, although considerably smaller than the one we were in. It transpired that a funeral party had booked the smaller hall, but with the loss of power there was nowhere for them to go. The manager had asked my da if the funeral party could set up in a corner of our hall. At first he objected, but then, out of respect, he agreed. What else could he do?

It put a dampener on the atmosphere. Well, for about half an hour. After that, Dot declared to the DJ, and anyone within earshot, 'Right they've had plenty of time to mourn. Get the music back on. Give us "Boom Bang a Bang" by Lulu.'

This went down like a lead balloon with the funeral party as the deceased had been killed in a gas explosion. A few minor scuffles broke out between mourners and wedding guests, resulting in the mourners leaving en masse. Being thrown out en masse is more accurate. Except, that is, for one of the granddaughters of the deceased who, after much toing and froing, was found in a storage cupboard with Dunky.

To this day Dorothy denies knowing about the gas explosion and claims that she simply wanted to hear her favourite record. I was always under the impression she hated Lulu, but maybe I was wrong.

With the funeral party gone the atmosphere improved considerably. The dance floor was never empty and there were plenty of drunken dads jiving as the forty-somethings relived their heyday. At one point I even saw Tony's granny sliding somebody through her legs and then enthusiastically doing the 'Twist'. You will remember the granny I'm talking about. Yes, you've got it: her that was on her last legs and deserved to sit at the top table before she went to meet her maker.

Donnie was dancing with Annie, a notable event in itself. Donnie didn't do dancing, not until he was in his late thirties. But that's a sight we will leave until much later, thank you very much. Annie, however, had insisted that he dance with her. It was their wedding day after all. She looked uncomfortable but very happy.

Until that is one of Tony's boisterous friends barged into her from behind and almost knocked her on top of Donnie. Annie let out a painful groan and grabbed her back. Donnie put his arm around her waist and gently coaxed her to a seat beside my ma. 'Keep your eye on her, will you Ma?'

He slowly walked across the dance floor and without further ado head-butted the guy who had just barged into them. As my da said earlier, let the games begin.

It was like the Wild West. There were chairs and bottles flying from one side of the room to the other, cries of 'Govan team, ya bastard' and retaliatory cries of 'KP star, ya bastard', these being the two local gangs.

From where I was sitting – between Annie and my ma – I could see at least four fights. Men were grappling with each other on the floor while their wives were pulling huge clumps of hair from the heads of their opponents and trying to kick shins with their lethal-looking stilettos.

This was my first wedding. It was brilliant. Every time I tried to get involved in the free-for-all, my ma grabbed me. 'Stay where you bloody are Danny. You're too wee for this nonsense.' But then I spied Charlie at the side of the stage being set upon by two of Tony's younger brothers. Not even my ma could keep me out of it now.

However, by the time I got there someone had pulled them apart, telling them to get to opposite sides of the stage. I think it was one of my aunties. As the two brothers walked away I noticed what looked like jelly and cream on their faces. I asked Charlie what had happened.

He grinned. 'When Donnie headed that guy and everybody started fighting, thae two were laughing. It was because Donnie went to kick another guy in the balls, missed, slipped on the dance floor and ended up on his arse. So when they laughed I smacked the two of them in the face with a bowl of trifle each.'

'Why?' I laughed.

'Because it was shite. The jelly was all watery and the custard was rotten.' He grinned his grin.

We sat on the stage and enjoyed the show. Donnie was going ballistic all over the hall. We saw him head-butt at least three guys and Dunky was right beside him throwing punches at anything that moved. Then I saw my da arguing with Tony's da. My da looked as if he was trying to calm Mr Murphy down. But Mr Murphy kept grabbing him and pointing at Donnie and Dunky, as if my da could stop them.

Eventually, my da gestured to Mr Murphy as if to say, 'Okay then, get the jackets off and let's fight if that's what you want.' Murphy started to take his jacket off, and when he had got his arms halfway up the sleeves, my da landed one on his jaw. The blow knocked him over a table and onto his back. It was sneaky from Da, but one to remember.

Meanwhile, Charlie was jumping up and down, cheering as if he was at a football match. He ran backwards and forwards along the stage, grabbing at people's hair when they came too close.

Dunky pushed a guy against the stage and was trying to get at him but his punches were being blocked by his opponent's defences. Then Charlie got involved. He pulled the guy's ears, causing him to scream. He tried to grab Charlie but that gave Dunky the chance to land a punch in his solar plexus. Then, when the guy folded over, Dunky kneed him in the face. He slid down the stage, holding his face with one hand and his stomach with the other.

'Cheers Charlie,' Dunky said, and then jumped on the back of a guy who was grappling with Donnie.

The lights in the hall suddenly came on at full power and the manager was on the stage, warning everyone that he had called the police. The party was over, he said. He wanted everybody out. That didn't go down too well and he exited the stage under a barrage of bottles and glasses.

The police arrived quarter of an hour later, by which time the fighting was dying out. However, that was not the only problem for the cops. The drunkest male guests – including Tony's da, although surprisingly not mine – even though they weren't involved in fisticuffs, couldn't stop shouting and swearing. And that was after being repeatedly told to stop by a young policewoman. This led to Tony's da and two of his uncles being huckled into the back of a police van.

These arrests were closely followed by the apprehension of Tony's granny by the constabulary. She had fallen and landed in an awkward position between a table and the wall. When a policeman tried to get her on her feet she bit his ear.

I noticed my ma gesturing to me to come over, so I grabbed Charlie and dragged him with me. I had to do it because he would have been next into the police van. He thought it was highly amusing to throw more trifle at the men who were being arrested. For some strange reason the policemen who were grappling with a bunch of drunks didn't find it as funny as Charlie.

As I dragged my little brother along, I heard him shout, 'Hey missus. I hope you are leaving some of thae sausage rolls for us.' Annie's mother was filling her handbag with what was left of the food. She looked affronted and moved away from the buffet table. 'Greedy old bastard,' was Charlie's considered opinion.

'Danny, come here,' my ma whispered loudly. 'Come here the both of you. Charlie you sit on your arse beside me and keep out of trouble, you bloody pest. Danny, go and find your da and Donnie. Tell one of them to phone an ambulance.'

When she saw my puzzled expression, she looked down at the floor at a puddle between Annie's feet.

'Annie's water's have broke.'

24

'It's a boy, Ma. It's a boy,' Donnie was shouting up at the window.

He was half drunk, as was Dunky. There might be a better or even a different way to celebrate apart from getting drunk. But we didn't know any.

'Will you look at them two prancing about in the rain for goodness sake,' my ma said to Dorothy, who was watching from the same window.

So there it was. The first McCallister grandchild. They called him Mark. He was a strapping lad of over seven pounds and Annie was beside herself with joy. If ever there was a woman intended for motherhood, it was her. Look up 'mother' in the dictionary and you will find a photo of Annie.

Mark's entry into the world was more dramatic than most. There had, of course, been the bar-room brawl at the wedding reception. Then Donnie ended up almost fighting with one of the ambulance-men when he cut the straps on Annie's stilettos. Annie went mental, screaming that they were her best shoes and had cost her three pounds.

When the ambulance guy explained that the straps had been cutting deep into her flesh, affecting her circulation, she was distinctly unimpressed. 'So fuckin' what. They cost me three quid you bastard. You can pay for them, so you can.' Years later, after her sixth child, she told me that she was always grumpy when she was in labour.

Annie and Mark came home six days later. The poor boy couldn't get a minute's peace. Everybody was at him. Between my ma, Dot and Darlene, I doubt if he was allowed to lie in his pram for more than an hour a day.

Mrs Wilson from the next close popped in to see him, declaring, 'You'll hurt his wee bones lifting him all the time.'

My ma was having none of it. 'Nonsense, cuddling never hurted a wean. Well it never hurted any of mine.'

But the wee man was left alone a bit more after that. Charlie would stand beside his pram for ages, staring at him. He was fascinated by his tiny fingers and nose. 'Look Danny,' he would say delightedly, pressing a finger into Mark's hand. Mark would grip it with all five fingers. 'Look how strong he is. He really grabs your hand. And he was smiling at me as well.'

'That's wind,' Darlene said, as she pushed Charlie aside, stuck her face into the pram and started baby talking: 'And where's my handsome wee man? And what are you saying today? Are thae smelly bad boys annoying you pal?' she cooed.

Mark woke with a start and let out a cry. It was no doubt because Darlene screamed, 'Ma gonny tell them,' when Charlie pulled her hair and twisted her ear.

'That's not fair,' Darlene was shouting. 'Why do I have to sleep in the kitchen? That's completely no' fair.'

'Darlene, shut up your whingeing. Tony's moving in with Dot today. How the hell can you sleep in the same room as them? Apart from anything else, they're going to be putting a cot in there for the wean,' my ma told her. Darlene was, as usual, in a strop.

'How can they not sleep in the kitchen? And I'll keep my room,' she complained.

That was a red rag to a bull for Dot. 'One more, Darlene. Go on. Say one more stupid bloody thing and I'll lamp you. I mean it Darlene. I don't even want to be here. I would have my own bloody house if Tony wasn't such a halfwit. So shut up and put the rest of your stuff in the hall cupboard like you were told.'

'And I'm not getting a cot yet Ma,' Dorothy continued. 'The council said I should have a house within four weeks. So the wean can just sleep in its pram until we get word, if we ever do. They're useless bastards down at the council.'

I don't know what Darlene was moaning about. Me, Charlie and Dunky were bedding down in the living room every night, because Donnie and Annie had taken our room. It would have been a nightmare if we had been getting up for school but luckily it was the summer holidays. Even so, Dunky and Donnie were fighting all the time because Dunky would be forever waking Annie and the wean up in the morning, looking for a pair of socks or his work boots.

It got too much for Donnie one night and he fairly laid into his brother. 'Is it too much to ask for you to get your stuff for work ready the night before Dunky, instead of waking them two up every bloody morning? They're already up at three o'clock and six o'clock for feeds. They don't need you waking them up again at half-seven.' They were standing toe-to-toe in the living room as Dunky as rolled out a sleeping bag for another night on the floor.

'Do you think you could maybe get a house sorted instead of us three sleeping on the floor?' was Dunky's not unreasonable response, although the look on his face was far from reasonable.

It would have escalated further if my da hadn't made it his business. 'Stop the shouting both of you. You're standing there moaning about Dunky waking the wean. Then you shout at the top of your voice and wake him up yourself,' he reproached Donnie.

He turned to Dunky. 'And this is my house, not yours. Don't you be bothering to tell anybody they shouldn't be here. And if I tell you to sleep on the floor, that's where you will sleep. Like it or lump it.'

Dunky was obviously debating with himself whether to continue the argument, because we had now been sleeping in the living room for a week. And since my ma wouldn't let any of us sleep on the new couch it was very uncomfortable. So he did have a point.

After all, Annie had been pregnant for nine months. It wasn't a shock. There had been plenty of time to sort out a house, so Dunky was right in a way. But he wisely decided not to continue the argument, especially not with my da. If it had only been Donnie, fair enough. But arguing with my da was unwise at the best of times. And this wasn't the best of times. Everybody was on top of everybody else, with arguments breaking out over trivialities.

The tension wasn't confined to the male members of the household. Dorothy had slapped Darlene the day before for going into what had been her own room and lying on the bed reading a magazine. 'Ma gonny tell her,' Darlene had screamed, as if she had been shot. The truth is Dorothy had barely touched her. She had slapped her, but a midwife slaps a newborn wean's arse harder than Dot slapped Darlene.

'She slapped me for nothing. I'm sick of this. Just because she's pregnant doesn't mean she can get away with murder. It's not my fault she's overdue and as fat as a bloody elephant. Why is she taking it out on me and slapping me in the face? She could ruin my looks. How am I going to be a model if she breaks my jaw? Gonny tell her?' Darlene ranted.

Darlene didn't need an excuse to be a drama queen and right now it was a daily occurrence. Bear in mind that my ma was now only a week short of her due date with her eighth child, which didn't make it any easier on her.

Da was taking the brunt of it because my ma blamed him for everything. It was his fault Donnie and Dunky were butting heads like a couple of young stags. It was his fault that Dot and Darlene were constantly hissing at each other like a couple of highly strung cats used to their own way. And it was probably his fault that baby Paul had the measles.

Paul was constantly crying because he was so itchy. No matter how you tied his wee mitts on he got them off again. He was also toddling now, so people were either tripping over him or taking drastic action to avoid him. If he was tied into his pram he would scream blue murder, because it felt like being in prison.

The only thing that wasn't my da's fault was that Charlie was acting up something rotten. The polis had been to the door twice because some old woman round in Middleton Street had complained about him kicking a ball against the wall of her house for hours on end. She said it annoyed the life out of her and her bedridden husband, whose bed was against the wall that Charlie used for football practice.

No, that wasn't my da's fault. That, miraculously, was my fault. If I would play football with Charlie, or occupy his time in some other way, then he wouldn't be annoying that old woman and her poor wee man. Nobody thought it was Charlie's fault. How could it be Charlie's fault? It was him that was doing it but it couldn't be his fault, not Charlie. See, even I was getting ratty.

25

'They've found me a house Ma,' Dorothy shouted, as she opened a letter from the council the very next day. 'I've to go and see it tomorrow. If we want it we can move in next week,' she gushed.

'*If* you want it?' my da interrupted, looking up from the *Evening Times* crossword. 'There's no *if* about it. You want it.'

'But what if it's a damp, stinking hovel Da? I canny just move into anywhere. It will need to be nice or I'm not taking it,' Dot said petulantly.

Sometimes she could be quite like Darlene, but don't tell her I said that.

'Dorothy darling, I don't care if it's in a back street in Calcutta or a cave in the Mongolian desert. You're taking it. You're moving as soon as I can get a van to put your stuff in,' my da said, in a pleasant tone but with a sarcastic smile.

In reality, Dorothy agreed with Da. She would move in anywhere just to have her own place and for the chance of building a nest for her overdue lump, as she called it.

Dorothy never got a chance to view the house. She went into labour that night, at two o'clock to be precise. Everybody was woken up by her shouting at her husband: 'Don't bloody start Tony. It's not cramp and it's not wind. My waters have broke. What did you think that wet patch was? Did you think I had pished myself?'

'It wouldn't be the first time, would it?' Tony shouted back.

'Aagh! Just go and get my ma you eejit. Move, and put some bloody trousers on. You're falling out of thae Y-fronts, you manky bastard.'

There was no need to go and get my ma. She was already up and was waking Darlene and Dunky. She told them to go down to the nearest phone box and call an ambulance. The nearest box was away along the Paisley Road, outside the Fountain bar. There was one closer, right across the road. But somebody – probably Charlie – had been trying to get the money. When the phantom raider couldn't get the coins out of it he bashed the handset against the steel frame of the box until it broke into pieces.

'We need to get a bloody phone in this house, Davie,' my ma said to my da.

'Aye that will be right,' he replied. 'Can you imagine the phone bills in here with all them, especially Darlene, yapping day and night?'

'Just for emergencies then. You could have a wee box next to it for people to put ten pence in when they make a call, like that Mrs Wilson in the next close,' she winced, holding her back as she struggled to get up from her chair.

'Aye and I bet she makes a few quid from it as well. Where are you going? Sit on your arse. You're not up to running after them,' my da responded.

'I'm not going anywhere. I'm getting some twinges,' she said, again wincing and holding her back.

'What kind of twinges?' my da asked, with a knowing look.

'I hope this ambulance is big enough for two. We're not long after a double wedding. Time for a double birth.'

Dot and my ma were laughing and wincing at the same time.

The ambulance arrived shortly afterwards. This time both my da and Tony decided to go along. My da said he was up anyway and he would put his working clothes on and go straight to work from the hospital.

My ma's reply was memorable. 'Okay David, so what time do you want us to start pushing these lumps out? Would six o'clock do you? Would that give you time to get to work? Maybe even time to stop and get your paper and a roll and sausage before you start. Six o'clock it is then? Do you hear that Dorothy? Start pushing at six o'clock. Your Da wants to get to work by seven.'

I think she was being sarcastic!

There was no room in the ambulance for any more than the expectant mothers, which meant that Tony and my da had to walk to the hospital. When Tony mentioned a taxi my da looked at him as if he had said, 'Let's burn some fivers to keep warm.'

'It's a couple of miles. It will take us about twenty minutes to walk it. Why would you want to spend good money on a taxi, you galoot? So that we can be there before the ambulance? What for? Do you think we will need to make the beds for them two to lie in? Why would we need to be there first? You do know they could spin this out for days, don't you?' he said, with barely concealed disdain.

I was glad my ma was already in the ambulance. She might have reacted badly to being accused of 'spinning out' childbirth.

Tony was shamefaced. 'I didn't think Davie. You're right. It would be a waste of money.' He made for the door.

'Tony,' my da said, 'do you maybe want to put some clothes on pal? I know it's supposed to be summer and all that but it's the middle of the night.'

Tony looked down at his Y-fronts and Dot's slippers, which covered his feet. 'Oh aye. Gimme a couple of minutes,' he replied, sheepishly.

'Can I come with you Da?' I asked.

'Why would you want to come, Danny? Hospitals are horrible places son. Most of the time they make you ill,' my da replied, shaking his head.

'I just want to. I can run round to the shops if you need anything or go and get tea from the machines. Darlene can look after Charlie and Paul. Go on Da. Let me come with you.'

'If he's coming then so am I,' Charlie said, petulantly. I knew it. The wee shite was going to spoil even this for me.

'For god's sake,' said my da. 'It will be like the bloody Clampetts. Why don't we get Donald and Dunky and Annie and the wean up as well?'

Then he looked at us and, for some unfathomable reason, said, 'Go and get dressed. But I mean it. One bit of nonsense and you will feel the rough side of my hand.'

The walk to the hospital was over in a flash. You couldn't say my da walked anywhere. He put his head down and his little legs scurried. He was relentless. Charlie and I were practically running to keep up. Tony ambled along, occasionally putting on a little spurt when he failed to keep up. One time he fell a couple of hundred yards behind and when he caught up he had two pints of milk in his hands. He handed one to my da.

'One of the benefits of being up early,' he explained.

My da took the milk: 'Maybe the people whose doorstep you nicked it from won't think that when they've got no milk for their porridge eh?' But Da drank it anyway, well most of it. He left me some.

'Look Da, a giant bag of rolls,' Charlie said, pointing to a black-bin-bag-full of morning rolls on the pavement outside a corner shop. 'Are you hungry?' he asked mischievously.

'See what you've bloody started,' my da said to Tony. 'These two think it's all right to thieve now, because of you knocking milk off of doorsteps. The first time any of them get lifted for thieving, you can pay their bloody fines boy.'

'I never nicked it off a doorstep. I nicked it off the milk float,' Tony said, his reasoning being that this made all the difference.

My da shook his head and turned to Charlie. 'Aye, Charlie, I'm hungry. But that doesn't mean I can help myself. The guy that runs that shop is the same as me. He's trying to earn a living and pay his bills, and he can do without toerags,' he cast a furious glance at Tony, 'stealing his stuff.'

Tony was oblivious to what my da was saying. In his world if something was there for the taking, you took it. If that made things hard for somebody else, tough luck. It was hard for everybody. His motto was every man for himself.

It was nearly daylight when we got to the hospital, which was starting to get busy. There were nurses everywhere, hurrying hither and thither. There were loads of vans, bread vans, greengrocers' vans. There was also a low, black van with the windows blacked out. When I asked my da what it was for he answered, 'Never mind that son.'

Tony smirked, 'That's for taking the dead bodies away Danny.'

'I know which dead body they might be taking away shortly,' my da said, glowering at Tony.

Charlie stood staring after the black van, obviously thinking the same as me: I wonder if there are dead people in there. And if there are, how did they die? Were they murdered, or were they in an accident? Or were they old people who breathed their last during the night.

Charlie asked, 'Where are they being taken at this time in the morning Da?'

My da again glanced at Tony, clearly not wanting an in-depth discussion on dead bodies at this time, or at any other time.

Tony explained: 'They are probably going to a funeral parlour to get embalmed and dressed up for their funeral. Unless they were murdered. In that case they will be going to the morgue for a post-mortem to get cut up and examined.' By telling Charlie this he had deliberately antagonised my da, which was never a wise move.

Charlie's eyes widened, not with fear but with interest. He really was a horrible wee shite.

'Enough Tony. You're frightening the weans,' my da ordered, misreading Charlie's expression.

26

The maternity department was heaving. There were pregnant women everywhere. They wandered about with dressing gowns on, waddling backwards and forwards like penguins with one hand holding their backs. Some were sitting and smoking a fag while staring out of the window, yearning to be out of this place or, perhaps more likely, yearning for something to be out of them.

We went to reception, where my da quietly asked a group of six nurses standing behind a circular desk where he could find my ma and Dorothy. They ignored him.

He asked again, and, when he was ignored for a second time, he said, in a louder voice, 'Listen, I'm sure your boyfriend didn't mean what he said hen. But do all of you need to ignore me and listen to her story? Would it not be better if just four of you ignored me and one of you answered my simple question? Where are Mrs Margaret McCallister and Mrs Dorothy Murphy?'

They turned around and looked at him as if he was something sticking to the soles of their shoes. But one of them realised he was not the sort who could be pushed too far. She stood at the counter, facing my da, and asked in a we're-busy-don't-bother-us tone of voice, 'When were the two ladies admitted?'

'They've just been brought in this morning by ambulance doll,' Tony interjected, leaning on the counter. He must have known her from somewhere. He had been staring at her since we arrived, focusing on the name badge that was pinned above her ample bosom. At least I think it was the name badge he was staring at!

'Oh aye, here they are down here. I couldn't read my own writing. They have been taken straight into the labour suite. If you would like to go along that corridor and have a seat in the waiting room, I'll see what I can find out.'

'And which one is the waiting room doll?' Tony asked, putting on what he thought was a suave tone.

'The one that says waiting room on the door pal. Maybe one of the weans can help you read it,' the busty nurse responded with a take-that smile.

My da glowered at Tony again but once again he shrugged his shoulders. 'I know, what a bitch. But what can you do?'

My da bristled. 'I'll tell you what I can fuckin' do,' and made a move towards Tony. But before he took a step a big fat nurse appeared.

Her name badge read Matron O'Malley and we soon heard her thick Irish brogue. 'Right the pair of you, enough of these shenanigans. There's two lovely girls through there trying to make you proud daddies and here's you two brawling like a couple of weans. And look at the two handsome young men behind you. They know how to behave themselves, even if you two don't. Now come away with you into the waiting room and I'll get one of this lot to bring some tea and toast.' These last words were spoken while she pointed at the nurses.

'Come on now,' O'Malley finished, with a stern look at my da who had another glower at Tony and then pushed him in the back towards the waiting room. Tony shook his head and stumbled, looking back over his shoulder with a hard-done-by look.

A few minutes later the nurse Tony had been staring at brought in a tray with four plastic cups of tea and a plate of toast. My da stared at his son-in-law so hard that he didn't even lift his head to have a sneaky look at her.

Two hours later the matron popped her head round the door. 'Mr McCallister, you have a fine healthy baby boy. He's weighing in at six pounds and three ounces. Mother and child are doing fine. You can go and see them in ten minutes.'

'Mr Murphy,' Matron O'Malley continued, frowning at Tony, 'you will have to wait a bit longer. Your little one likes it fine where he is. The doctor's going to come and have a look at your wife. She's a wee bit uncomfortable. It looks like a big yin if you ask me.'

Tony turned a full shade paler and nodded. I don't know whether he was worried about the baby being okay or how Dorothy was going to treat him if she had to endure a lot of pain. Because we all knew that, whatever happened, it would be his fault. On reflection, I think he was more worried about what Dot might do to him.

My ma was sat up on the hospital bed. She looked a bit tired but, apart from that, okay. The baby was in her arms, wrapped in a shawl. 'What are thae two doing with you Davie?' she asked my da, but smiling at us anyway.

'Come up and see boys,' she said, adjusting the bundle in her arms.

Charlie leapt onto the bed. 'Careful wee man,' my da said, grabbing him before he landed on top of my ma and the baby. I walked around the bed, to where I could get a view of him.

'That's your wee brother Charlie,' my ma said, putting one hand on Charlie and pulling him closer to kiss the top of his head, 'and yours as well, of course, Danny.'

'This is rubbish. I've already got a wee brother. I wanted a wee sister,' Charlie moaned.

'You're right. I've got two wee brothers and it's really terrible,' I laughed.

My da smiled and pulled me towards him. 'Not all the time Danny. Not all the time son.'

Meanwhile, in the background, and at full volume, we heard: 'Tony, you bastard. Wait till I get back on my feet. This is fucking sore. Tony, you bastard, just you wait.'

'That sounds like our Dorothy,' my ma said to my da, and we all laughed.

'I wouldn't want to be Tony right now,' Charlie grinned.

'You wouldn't want to be Tony at any bloody time,' my da responded, and he wasn't joking.

My ma told my da to take Charlie and me home and make sure we got something to eat and a wee lie down. They were also thinking about Darlene. She would be frantic. It had been hours since we left the house.

'No, it's okay. I got Danny to phone Mrs Wilson's with the news about this one,' my da said, by now holding the baby in his arms.

'What are we doing about a name for him? We can't keep calling him "this one",' my ma pointed out.

Charlie offered his opinion 'He could be Peter, after Peter McCloy, the Rangers goalkeeper. Or Colin, after big Colin Jackson, the Rangers centre half. Or Kai, after Kai Johansen, the Rangers right back.'

'We get the drift Charlie. But we're not calling him after a football player,' my ma said, a smile playing on her lips.

'What about the whole team then? You could call him Peter, Kai, Colin, John, Alex . . . .' Charlie suggested, mischievously.

'Enough Charlie. He's not getting called after the Rangers team. What if I want to call him after the Celtic team? How would that be wee man? Do you fancy that?' my ma asked, laughing at the look of horror on Charlie's face. Ironically, Charlie later became an ardent Celtic fan.

'What about David?' I asked, almost whispering.

My ma raised her eyebrows and looked at my da. 'Well,' she said.

My da interrupted, shook his head and said in a quiet voice, 'No we can't do that.' He had a strange look on his face, which I didn't understand.

'How not?' I asked. 'Lot's of my pals are called after their da.'

'It will probably be our last one Davie. I'm getting too old for this now. We're getting too old for this now,' my ma sighed, reaching out and taking my da's hand.

I was lost. There was something going on here and I wasn't getting it. What could possibly be wrong with calling the wee man David? Although when I thought about it, it was more common to call the first son after his father.

'What's the matter Ma?' Charlie asked, noticing a tear running down her face.

Thinking about my theory regarding first-born sons I asked, 'How come Donald wasn't called after you Da? How come he was called Donald and not David? He should have been called David, the same as you. You are the oldest in your family and you're called David after my Granda McCallister. So how come Donald is Donald and not David?'

My ma looked at my da and he nodded. 'Come up here beside me Danny,' my ma said, patting the bed. Charlie was already on the bed beside her. My only surprise was that he wasn't under the covers with her.

I sat beside her. She took my hand and Charlie's hand. My da stood watching, the baby in his arms. Ma smiled: 'Donald wasn't your first big brother. He had a big brother as well. He died you see, when he was just a wee baby like this one.'

Charlie was horrified and I must have had the same expression. We looked at the bundle in my da's arms with dread.

My ma was quick to clarify what she meant. 'Oh no boys. I'm sorry. I don't mean he was the same. He wasn't. He was very, very wee and not well at all. He was born too early, premature the doctors call it. He never really had a chance the poor wee soul. But the thing is he was called David, so . . . .'

My da looked at my ma. 'Maggie maybe we can call this wee yin Davie as well hen. After all he will be the last,' and then added with a smile. 'Maybe . . . .'

It made my ma smile. 'No maybes Davie. That gorgeous wee boy in your arms is the last. I'm too tired for more, really I am.' And, right at that moment, she looked it.

We went back to the waiting room to find Tony, who was leaning against a wall with his back to us. As we got nearer we could see that there was someone talking to him. But we couldn't see who, because he was blocking our line of sight. It was only when we got close that we saw it was the nurse from earlier on.

My da took hold of Tony's arm and turned him around until his back was against the wall: 'You, you wee tart. Get out of my fuckin' sight before you get me angry.'

The nurse opened her mouth to say something but the look on my da's face put her right off. She got out of there at a fair old clip. She wasn't running but neither was it a stroll in the park.

'Tony my boy. We need to have a word,' Da said, dragging him into the gents' toilet, which was about five yards away. Tony's feet didn't touch the floor.

My da thrust something into my hand and said 'Subway, now!' Then they abruptly disappeared into the gents. I looked down at my hand and found two ten-pence pieces.

'Right Charlie. Let's go and get a couple of Marathons in case we get hungry on the walk home,' I said, flipping one of the coins and catching it.

It was nine o'clock that night before my da came home. He smelled as if he had come home via a brewery. 'Dorothy had a wee boy as well sweetheart,' he said, holding on to Darlene to keep from falling over.

'I'm a daddy and a granda on the same day. That takes a bit of beating, eh? The boys in the pub helped me to wet the babies' heads, both of them. I mean both weans. I don't mean one of them had two heads. Och, you know what I mean hen. Dorothy had a wee boy as well, you know,' he continued, his arm still around Darlene.

'We know,' Darlene told him, slipping sideways from under his arm, which caused him to stumble and put his hand against the wall for support. 'Tony came home at four o'clock and said that Dorothy had a wee boy and he told us about my ma. How could you? How could you go and get steaming and leave her there to die? How could you?' she screamed.

I have never seen anyone sober up so quickly.

'What, what are you talking about? Dying? What the fuck are you talking about? Answer me, you stupid lassie. Answer me,' Da raged.

'My ma could have died and you just left her there on her own. How could you? Just so you could get drunk. How could you? I hate you,' she screeched, slamming her room door behind her.

As Darlene stormed off, Annie emerged from the kitchen. 'Boys, into your room and into your beds, now. Go, move it!' she ordered, clapping her hands to emphasise the urgency.

We did but we could still hear every word. 'Davie, Maggie was in a bad way. After you left she haemorrhaged. It was touch and go. They gave her loads of transfusions and that. And they had to do an emergency hysterectomy. Oh Davie, I thought we had lost her.'

Annie broke down. We could see through the crack in the door she was on her knees at my da's feet, sobbing her heart out.

My da stood still, a stunned and uncomprehending look on his face. He was in shock. 'I don't understand hen. What are you saying to me? Is your ma okay?'

Donald had come out of the kitchen, just behind Annie. 'The doctors think she will be all right Da. But she was in a really bad way. Where the fuck were you?' The last part was said in an accusing tone.

It broke my da's heart.

He sobbed, just once, and said: 'I was in Partick. I went for a pint with your uncle Charlie and my pals. Is that a crime? Is it?' he bawled.

Then his tone changed completely. He spoke softly. 'My wife, your ma, gave birth to my seventh son today. She told me she wanted to call him after me. Wee Davie, that's his name now. I went to celebrate. I also went to celebrate my beautiful wee lassie Dorothy giving me another strapping wee grandson. What did I do that was so bad, eh? Why are you looking at me like that? Tell me what I did.' He was sobbing. Then he turned his back on us and went out the front door.

'I'm going to the hospital.'

27

It was nearly a week later that Dorothy got out of hospital. My da had been drunk for the biggest part of that week. He talked to no one and we tried to avoid talking to him. Saying anything was asking for trouble. He even threw one of his shoes at me when I asked if he wanted a cup of tea. He threw the other one at Annie when she told him he needed to eat something; that he couldn't survive on lager and whisky.

He also tried to punch Donald when he told him how the foreman at their job asked when he was coming back to work. It was only because he was so drunk, and could hardly stand up, that none of his wild swipes at Donald connected. Donald was able to manhandle him into his room and let him fall on the bed, cursing and threatening more violence.

'You're not too big yet, Donnie. As soon as I get off this bed I'm going to batter you. You think you're a big man, don't you?' he slurred.

He went on, in his most sarcastic tone: 'Big Donnie McCallister, the hard man. He thinks he can take his da. Well you canny son, no' yet, no' ever. I'll show you who the big man is. Don't you bloody worry, I'll show you.' He lay back on the bed and slipped into a drunken sleep, still muttering, and weakly flailing his arms. 'Hard man is it? I'll show you hard man.'

Donnie was in tears as he walked away.

'He's been like that for a week Dot. I don't know what to do with him. He gets up in the morning and stomps about, banging doors and kicking things out of his way. Then he leaves without getting washed or nothing. He stinks like an old jakey. I really don't know what to do with him Dot. I really don't,' Annie said, wringing her hands in despair.

'Me and my ma aren't daft you know Annie. We knew something

was up. Why didn't you tell us he was like this instead of saying he was working overtime and couldn't come to the hospital to see my ma? We could maybe have done something,' Dorothy said, clearly exasperated.

Annie stood up her full five feet two inches. 'Is that right Dot? What exactly could you have done? Your ma's still no well after losing all that blood and you've just had a hard time yourself having the wean. So what should I have said, eh?

'Should I have said, "Dorothy, you better come home and look after your drunken old da?"

'Or, "Right Maggie. On your feet, and stop acting it. Your alcoholic husband needs you. Never mind your newborn or the six pints of blood you lost. Come on now, on your feet. Rise and shine."

'So, which one should it have been Dot? You or your ma? Tell me which one?'

Dorothy looked aghast at Annie and then smiled. 'Rise and shine Maggie. Aye that would have worked.' They burst out laughing, maybe just to stop them from greeting.

When they stopped laughing Dorothy said, 'I'm home now and my ma is coming home in two days. I'll be putting his gas at a peep tomorrow. You wait and see. He can like it or lump it but this house is getting back to normal before my ma comes home. Trust me.'

I thought I was first up the next morning. I went into the kitchen intending to clean and set out the fire in case it needed to be lit later on. One of the many women in our house always seemed to be freezing, even in summer. Annie and Dorothy were both sitting at the kitchen table feeding their babies. Dorothy was bottle-feeding Anthony junior while Annie was breast-feeding wee Mark.

'Put the tea out Danny,' Dot said. The past week had been so awful I was happy to be hearing the kettle whistling away in the background.

I had barely poured their tea, and buttered Annie's toast, when we heard a banging coming from my ma and da's room. 'Where's my fuckin' boots, Darlene? What have you done with my boots?' my da shouted.

Dorothy looked at Annie and smirked.

My da came into the kitchen; 'What one of youse has moved my boots? I had them on last night. Where are they?' He was almost shouting.

'Da, wee Anthony's falling asleep. Could you keep it down? And your boots are put away,' Dorothy told him.

'What does that fuckin' mean, put away?' my da whisper-shouted.

Dorothy smiled. 'That means they have been put where you canny get them. You're not going out today. In fact, you won't be going out until tomorrow when we go to get my ma.'

My da said sarcastically, 'Oh here we go. Maggie's wee lassie thinking she can tell her old da what to do. Well I'll put my good shoes on. They're in the wardrobe. Ha, there you go.'

'They're put away as well,' Dorothy said, smugly, 'and so are your slippers and even your wellies and that old pair of golf shoes. So if you want to go out it will be in your bare feet. Ha, so there you go as well.'

Annie was struggling to suppress her laughter. 'Well bare feet it is then,' he said triumphantly. 'It won't be the first time. I used to walk to school in my bare feet.'

'I know Da, through two feet of snow wasn't it?' Dot snorted, derisively. 'We've heard the stories. But tell me. Did you ever try to walk down stairs and out of a close that was covered in tacks in your bare feet?' Dot asked, with a huge grin.

'You wouldn't.' He looked at me and said, 'Danny son . . . .'

I don't know what he was going to ask. Maybe to find him footwear or to clear the tacks, although in reality there were no tacks. But before he could speak, I jumped up and skirted past him.

'Late for school Da. Need to move.'

Charlie, who had come into the kitchen behind my da, wondering what the commotion was, said, 'Me too Da, sorry,' and sprinted after me.

Charlie and I stood in the hall, listening to what followed.

'My ma gets out tomorrow, Da. She's not completely right yet. The last thing she needs is you being steamboats all the time. So get dressed, go to work and bloody grow up. Just this once, she needs you Da. She's still not well and I think she got a bit of a fright. And wee Davie's a cracker Da. You've not seen very much of him. He's got blond hair. It's nearly pure white,' Dot said. She had started off angrily but by the end of her little speech she was almost pleading.

'Just like his da then. My hair's nearly pure white, what's left of it that is. Do you not think I got a fright as well? She's a moaning-face wee bastard but what would I do without her? I canny even find my boots and I didn't know I had old golf shoes. I must take that up again just to get away from you lot. Fair enough I'll give the drink a miss for a while, till your ma gets back on her feet. And, by the way, Dot, it's all very well telling me to grow up. But you've a big bit of that to do yourself, hen, with that new wean to look after. Let's see how easy you think it is in twenty years. Just you wait and see. And come back in twenty years and tell me how easy it was,' my da said quietly.

As he emerged from the kitchen and spotted us he swatted at Charlie's behind. 'Move it you two. I thought you said youse were away to school.'

'We are Da,' I replied. 'We are. We were waiting for Dot to make us a play-piece.'

My da smiled. 'Here, there's two bob each. Get something for you and Charlie's play-piece out of the shop. Just move your arses now, away to school.'

As we left Charlie said: 'How come he gets my money as well as his, Da? You could have gave me the two bob myself. Or do you think I need to grow up a bit first?' He burst out laughing and quickly closed the door behind us.

28

We had to go to school the next day and the following day as well. No amount of pleading would make either Dot or my da change their minds. In fact my da went to work as well, even though my ma was coming home that afternoon. He told Dot he was going in because the foreman on the job was being a bit of a prick about the time he had taken off recently. And anyway, Dot and Darlene were there to look after my ma. He would just be in the way.

'I feel as if I'm going to be sick any minute miss. My stomach's rumbling and really sore. I don't think I can go back to the classroom miss. Maybe you should send me home miss. It's nearly two o'clock anyway miss. Aargh, my belly is sore.' I was putting it on as much as I could but acting wasn't my strong suit. I looked pleadingly at the school nurse.

'Well it's probably something you ate Daniel. And whatever it was, your wee brother Charlie must have eaten it as well. He's sitting outside at the front door, waiting for somebody to take him home. Do you think if I let you go home as well, that you can manage to take him with you? Or are both of you so sick that I should maybe get an ambulance to take you home? Or better still to take you to the Southern General, just in case these sore bellies are life-threatening.' She had seen through the pretence.

I put my head down, unsure what to say after being so easily caught out.

'Away you go Danny and get Charlie on the way out. By the way, tell your ma I was asking for her and I hope to see her down the pub as soon as she is back on her feet.'

The nurse grinned when she saw the wide-eyed look of surprise on my face.

'It's today she gets home from the hospital isn't it? Go on. Go home and take the pest with you. I take it you two didn't plan this. He told me he had a sore stomach because someone had poisoned him and he had to go home while the house was empty and look for evidence. I suppose we can rule out the poisoning theory then. Go on Daniel. Off with you. And close your mouth or you'll be catching flies,' she said, smiling broadly.

Darlene wasn't exactly pleased to see us.

'What are you two doing home? You better get in that room and stay out of the way. My ma's coming home in an hour and we are trying to have it nice for her. Why are you two home anyway? We've been cleaning this house all day and you two better not bring in any dirt in. I mean it. If you leave one bit of dirt anywhere you will be getting it, I'm telling you. And Paul has been greeting all morning and that's started off wee Anthony and wee Mark. It's been mental in here with three weans greeting and Dot shouting. And why are you home anyway?'

'Calm down and breathe Darlene. If you let me get a word in edgeways, I'll tell you. We got sent home because the boiler broke down and there's no heating,' I said convincingly.

'No heating Daniel. Now why would the school need heating on at the beginning of June? Danny, have you moved school from Ibrox primary to Alaska primary?' Dorothy asked, coming out of the kitchen with little Anthony in her arms and Paul hanging on to her skirt.

'I didn't decide to send everybody home. It's not up to me is it?' I said, all flustered.

'No it isn't Danny. I'll ask Agnes Simpson when I see her who made the decision. You know Agnes Simpson, don't you Danny? She's the school nurse. Now if Agnes tells me you two are dogging it, that would be a different story Danny, wouldn't it?' Dot said knowingly.

Charlie decided he had the solution to our dilemma: 'I heard she might be getting the sack, that school nurse. The way I heard it, she has been sending people home for no reason and then saying they made up a story about being no' well. She just grabs wee boys and lassies and says, "Right you're going home, move it." I heard she was doolally, probably sniffing the fumes off that nit lotion.'

The only ones not there when my ma came home in a taxi at half past four were Donnie and my da. Within two minutes of my ma sitting in the armchair at the fire, Dorothy was telling us to give her some room and let her breath.

'For Christ's sake Charlie. Get off my ma's neck. You're like a wee human scarf. Daniel, you as well. There isn't room on that chair for you and my ma. Go and sit on the couch. In fact, go and make my ma a cup of tea,' Dorothy said, grabbing at Charlie with one arm, while she held onto her baby with the other. Surprise, surprise, I had to go and make the tea.

'I don't understand what all the fuss is for anyway. I've had plenty of weans before. Why are you three not at school? And Dunky, why are you not at work?' my ma asked, wincing as she tried to get comfortable on the chair, now that neither Charlie nor I were attached to her.

Dunky opened his mouth to explain but, before he could, Darlene's mouth got into top gear. 'I'm not at school because Dot kept me off to tidy up for you coming home and to help look after Paul. Dunky was at work all day. He came home at four because he started early this morning, so he could finish a wee bit earlier this afternoon. And thae two pests,' pointing at Charlie and me, 'aren't at school because either the school nurse has had a nervous breakdown or Charlie's a wee liar. And when they came home early, they never even helped to tidy their room or anything. I've done just about everything myself the day. And Paul's been greeting all day. He must be missing you and him greeting woke the two babies up all day and . . . .'

This was too much for my ma. 'Ok Darlene, I get it. Give your mouth a wee rest hen. It's done more work than the rest of you put together. You're a good lassie but you canny half talk. Go and bring my bag in from the hall. Annie went yesterday and got you a pair of earrings, from me, for looking after everybody while I was in hospital.'

Darlene leapt out to the hall and rushed back in holding the earrings up to the window to see them better. She held them at her ears while looking in the mirror above the fireplace.

'These are for pierced ears and my ears aren't pierced,' she smiled, anticipating what my ma would say next.

'Dorothy's going to pierce your ears later on. You're old enough now, I suppose,' my ma said, to Darlene's obvious delight.

'I've been old enough for ages. Can I start wearing makeup as well? Even a wee bit of mascara and lipstick? Can I Ma?' she asked eagerly.

Dorothy answered: 'You better not be touching any of my makeup hen. You can start wearing makeup when you can afford to buy it. That's what I think. And I'll be having thae hot pants back by the way, while I remember.'

'You'll never get your fat belly in thae hot pants again. They're mine now and I wouldn't be seen dead in that bright red lipstick you wear. You look like a tart with that stuff on. I'll be getting nice pale-pink lipstick and blue eye shadow to enhance my high cheek bones and accentuate the fullness of my lips. And a black mascara to lengthen my eyelashes. If you want to be a model you need to think about these things, not just slap everything on as if you're painting the living-room ceiling,' Darlene said haughtily, and walked out of the living room admiring her reflection in the mirror as she went.

'She talks such a lot of crap,' Charlie said as he turned the TV on and sat on the floor, directly in front of the screen.

My ma laughed and tried to get up. 'This isn't getting your da's supper on, is it?' she said, putting both hands on the armchair to push her up.

'Sit down. What the hell do you think you're doing? He could make his own bloody supper for once. But he doesn't have to and neither do you. Annie has made some mince and totties. The mince is on a low peep and as soon as he comes in the totties can go on. You just sit down. You've got to rest Ma. That's a big thing you've just went through. You need to look after yourself and bugger the rest of them. They can all look after themselves,' Dorothy instructed, gently pushing my ma back into the chair.

'Well I can't sit here doing nothing. Go and bring me the totties hen and I can sit here and peel them.'

'For goodness sake woman. Would you just do as you're told? The totties are all done and you need to take it easy. Sit there and don't move. Charlie, put something on the telly your ma likes,' Annie said.

Frustrated, Charlie said, 'Do you want to watch Bill and Ben? Or will I turn it over to *Crackerjack* Ma?'

'We will watch *Crackerjack* Charlie. That Bill and Ben are nearly as hard to understand as Darlene is.'

Charlie thought this was hilarious. He rolled about the floor laughing, 'Ha ha. Darlene with Bill and Ben. That would be a good yin. Even Bill and Ben talk more sense than her.'

29

It was six o'clock and time for my da to come home. When we heard the front door open and close, we presumed it was him.

'Gimme him and go and put the totties on Annie hen,' my ma said, motioning to Annie to give her little Mark over.

'I'll put him in his pram in the hall, Maggie. He's just about falling asleep anyway,' Annie smiled.

We heard her muttering something in the hall, then raising her voice slightly. It sounded like, 'Go and tell her then.'

Donnie came into the living room, looking sheepish.

'Where is he away to?' my ma asked. 'The pub I suppose?' answering her own question, with a look of mild disgust, but no real surprise.

'He said he won't be long,' Donnie replied apologetically, shrugging his shoulders. 'He has went for a beer with George Davidson, the foreman. The two of them have been arguing all day about . . . .'

He looked at my ma, wondering how much she knew about the time off my da had taken in the last couple of weeks.

'And he thought that was more bloody important than coming home and seeing my ma,' Dorothy shouted at Donnie.

'Don't shout at me. I'm not his keeper. Since when could I tell my da what to do? If he wants to go for a pint he'll go for one. I can't stop him. Are you daft? Anyway Ma, how are you? I'm glad you're home. Maybe you can settle my da down a bit. He's been biting the head off everybody. I thought he was going to lamp George today. The two of them were right into it,' Donnie responded, before going over to my ma and giving her a peck on the cheek.

'I'm feeling a bit better now son. Still a wee bit sore at my belly but that will pass. Your Da's right. He can't afford to lose his job and if he has to go for a pint with that wee nyaff Davidson then so he should. I'm sure he will be in shortly. Annie put the totties on. If big Davie's not in when they're ready, we can have our supper and put his in the oven,' my ma said.

She didn't believe he would be in shortly any more than the rest of us.

* * *

Charlie woke me up.

'What time is it?'

'Charlie, why are you waking me up? Is it time for school?

'No, it's eleven o'clock at night. I can hear my da shouting. I'm scared.'

'He's not shouting at you. Put your head under the blanket and go to sleep,' I said, doing just that myself. Charlie pulled the blanket back and got in underneath it with me.

'Go and see what he's doing Danny,' he implored.

'No, why should I get a slap? Let somebody else see what he's doing. I'm going to sleep.' I pulled the blanket over our heads once again.

'Please Danny. Go and see. He's drunk. Go and see. He won't hit you. Go and see. Please Danny, please.'

There was no way Charlie was going to let me go back to sleep. I slipped out of the bed in my vest and pants and told him to stay where he was and keep quiet. I didn't want my da hearing anything and turning on us.

'I can go for a fuckin' drink whenever I fuckin' want. I'm the man of this house and don't you forget it. What I say goes. I'm sick of you fuckin' telling me what to do. I'm not working all day to come home to dried-up muck for my dinner. What sort of man has to sit in his bedroom and eat his dinner for Christ sake?'

My da was angry but not shouting at the top of his voice. Perhaps he was sober enough to realise that the three prams he had passed in the hall belonged to newborn babies who would be sleeping peacefully at this time of night. Although perhaps not.

The door of my parents' bedroom was slightly ajar. I could see the wall beside the door. There was mince and totties running down it from above the light switch. There was also a broken plate lying on the floor.

My ma answered him: 'I know Davie. I'm sorry. Just calm down. The three boys are sleeping in the living room and Darlene is sleeping in the kitchen alcove. There's nowhere else for you to eat your dinner this late.'

My da was on that in a flash: 'What do you mean this late? Have I got a certain time I need to be in for? Who do you think I am? Dunky or Danny? Or, more to the point, who do you think you are telling me to be in early if I want fed, eh? Who the fuck do you think you are?' he ranted, without raising his voice.

'Please Davie. You'll wake the weans. Please. I'm sorry. I wasn't saying you couldn't go for a drink when you wanted. I was just asking how it went with George Davidson. Is everything okay now?' my ma asked in a conciliatory tone.

'No, it fuckin' isn't okay. I battered that wee shite outside the Viceroy tonight. So I probably haven't even got a job. Are you happy now? I've not got a fuckin' job and all you do is keep having more fuckin' weans. Look at the state of this place with shitey nappies. I can hardly sit down in here without sitting on a fuckin' rattle or a dummy tit.'

I felt a prod in my back: 'They're not all my ma's weans,' Darlene whispered. 'Go and wake Dot up. She'll tell him.'

'You go and wake Dot up. Why is it always me that has to get shouted at?' I asked, when it was clear Darlene wasn't going anywhere.

'Oh don't Davie. I'm not well. Please don't,' my ma screamed.

But before I could react, Dot burst out of her room, closely followed by Tony in his Y-fronts.

'Leave it Dot, just leave it,' Tony was saying, hanging on to Dot's arm.

'No fuckin' way. He's not getting away with it this time,' Dot replied, with grim determination. Then she spotted Darlene and me, and shouted, 'Go to bed you two. Right now. Get to bed.'

Darlene was sobbing. 'He's gonny hit her Dorothy. Don't let him hit her. Please. She's just out of hospital. Dot, please stop him.'

My da opened the bedroom door wide. I scuttled out of his way intending to duck back into the living room. Darlene screamed with fright at the force he had used to pull open the door.

'What the fuck are you screaming for? Get to your bed. Don't sit listening at bloody doors. Go on, get to your bed,' Da bellowed.

'Darlene, go to your bed hen. Everything's fine. Your da's just tired. Go on, get to bed,' my ma said, appearing from behind my da. She was standing in a housecoat and slippers and had obviously just been woken up. She looked very tired.

'Don't you bloody apologise for me. Do you hear me?' my da shouted. My ma winced and shrunk away from him, as he lifted his hand.

Dorothy threw herself between them, 'Come into my room Ma. You need to watch what you're doing. You'll burst your stitches, so you will.'

As Dot led my ma towards her bedroom she cast a contemptuous look at my da, which he noticed. It enraged him, because he aimed a swipe at Dot. But, before he could connect, Tony had grabbed his arm.

'I don't think so Davie,' Tony warned him. 'I might not hit back when you have a go at me. But lift your hand to my wife and I will. Go to your bed Davie. It's late and the weans are up and getting upset. Please leave it and go to bed.'

My da, struggling to free his arm, was fumimg. 'I'll wake my Donnie up. He'll sort you out, you wee diddy. Donnie will knock your head off if I wake him up.'

'No, he won't Da. Go to your bed and give us peace,' Donnie said, from his bedroom door, before slamming it shut.

It was all quiet the next day when I went to school. Neither of my parents was awake when I got up and I had great difficulty getting Charlie up. His view was that if either my ma or my da wanted us to go to school then they would have got us ready. It took me twenty minutes and a fist fight to persuade him to get dressed. I knew that if he was still there when my da got up, he would be sorry.

As it turned out he was more right than I was. When Charlie and I got home at half-past three, the house was unnaturally quiet. Darlene was sitting in the kitchen with Dot and Annie. All three had a baby in their arms. 'Thank god you're home Danny,' Annie said gravely.

'Why, what's the matter?' I said, panicking.

'We're all dying for a cup of tea,' she cackled. With that, she pulled me to her by the collar with one hand, while holding the baby in her other arm, and kissed me on the cheek.

'You're a wee lifesaver. Get the kettle on,' she giggled.

I wiped my cheek and, smiling, said, 'Stop slobbering all over my face or I won't be making you tea ever again.'

Charlie posed the question I had been thinking about since we got home.

'Where's my ma and da?'

'My ma's having a wee lie down. She was up but was a bit tired. So she's away back to bed,' Dorothy answered.

'And where's my da?' Charlie asked again.

'Who cares?' Dot replied.

'He's in his bed as well,' Darlene said. 'He was up first thing. I heard him in the toilet being sick. But he hasn't come out of his room since then. Probably got a hangover.'

'More likely ashamed of himself and scared to show face,' Dorothy said angrily, and not in a quiet voice. If the bedroom door was open, he would have heard her.

'Shush,' Annie said. 'He'll hear you. Don't get him started again.'

'He won't start again. He's sober. Well, just about sober. And he's not so quick at lifting his hands when he's sober,' Dorothy said again, not lowering her voice one iota.

'Dorothy, please don't get it all going again. The weans are unsettled. Please leave it be,' Darlene begged.

Dot nodded, indicating her agreement, but mumbled, 'This is why he does it. Because he thinks nobody will say anything. He thinks we're all scared. Well I'm not bloody scared of him.'

Annie said, 'Maybe you should be. It's gonny be another week before Tony gets the decorating finished in your new house. You don't want your da throwing you out just yet, do you?'

'I suppose so,' Dot replied. 'But, come to think of it, that lazy article has had over a week to decorate the house. What's taking him so long?'

'Well your da was supposed to be helping him but he's been pished for a fortnight. So unless you wanted your wallpaper upside down it's just as well Tony did it on his own. He has been at it the full week you know. It's a sin. He's hardly had any time to do his hair and makeup neither he has,' Annie said, guffawing at her own joke. She liked her own jokes did Annie.

Dorothy had a point. Whenever my ma and da had a fight it was forgotten about the next day. Nobody mentioned it. We crept about on eggshells for a few days and hoped the next one would be a long time in coming.

Only the bruises and black eyes lasted more than a day or two.

30

Tony was nearly six feet tall, which was a good ten inches taller than Dot. So they looked odd when you saw them together. He wasn't a bad guy but he was shorter than Dot when it came to common sense. Sometimes Tony couldn't see the wood for the trees. His heart was mostly in the right place though. He did love Dot in his own way. It's just that his way often didn't make much sense.

There was a time before they were married that Dot was told that somebody had seen Tony kissing a lassie outside the Jester pub on Paisley Road. When Dot pulled him up he didn't deny it. His excuse was that the lassie fancied him and told him that she was a much better kisser than Dot. So, to defend Dot's honour, Tony spent twenty minutes winching this lassie to prove her wrong. He told Dot this with a straight face and was staggered she couldn't see he had only done it to protect her reputation.

Imagine his surprise when Dorothy tried to stab him with a pair of toenail scissors!

'Keep your knickers on. How am I supposed to do all that in a week, and work all week as well? You are a right eejit sometimes,' Tony said to Dot, half joking.

Charlie, Darlene and I had invited ourselves along to have a nosey at Dot's new house. As we were walking along Govan Road pushing three prams – baby Anthony, baby David and toddler Paul – Dot had a playful go at Anthony about all the things she was expecting to have had done to the house. 'Well, at the very least, every room better be painted and papered.'

'Every room, are you sure Dot? It's a room-and-kitchen after all,' Tony laughed.

Dot went along with the joke. 'You know what I mean. I wanted every bit of skirting board and ceilings painted and all the walls papered. And if there was any damp I wanted distemper on the walls first. If there's one bit of damp, your face is getting rubbed in it. I'm not taking my beautiful wee Tony into a damp house.'

'I'm not that wee. But do you really think I'm beautiful?' Tony asked, with a cheesy grin,

'Not you. Baby Tony, you halfwit!' Dot laughed.

It was to be a running joke with Tony that whenever anybody said anything complimentary about the baby, he would ask: 'Do you mean me?' He never tired of this joke. But we did, very quickly.

The house was in a part of Govan known as Wine Alley. The reason for the name was obvious to Glaswegians and it wasn't because it reminded you of French vineyards. It was a collection of slum streets. There were one or two pockets of resistance where the front gardens, so called, weren't full of old washing machines, rusty bike parts and broken bed frames, with and without minging mattresses.

We hardly noticed the state of the place. After all, we had lived in a similar environment in McLean Street, before moving to Cessnock Street. Yes there were slums here and some of the people were scumbags. But there were plenty of decent people who couldn't afford any better. Others had lived here for years and didn't want to move. They were living in the past, when things had been so much better. They were hopeful that the place could be turned around and returned to what it once was.

The close we stopped at when Tony announced 'this is it' looked reasonable enough. Their flat was on the second floor and the residents of the two flats on the ground floor looked as if they maintained their wee bits of front garden quite well. In fact, in one of the gardens there was an elderly couple sitting on kitchen chairs around a beat-up coffee table. The elderly woman said something, but as she had no teeth so she spoke with a pronounced lisp.

'Are thu all moofin in ere?' she asked.

'Are youse all moving in there?' her husband translated.

'Oh no. Just me and the tall streak of piss,' Dot giggled, pointing at Tony. 'Oh aye and my wean, wee Anthony,' she added, with obvious pride.

'Shoe ill ike it ere.'

'You will like it here' the old man clarified.

'Thith ith wan of the bether clotheth,' the old woman went on.

Dot held her hand up. 'One of the better closes. Aye, I get it,' before the old gentleman had a chance to translate.

'Well I better get up the stairs and see what mess my man has made of the decorating,' Dot said, eager to see what had been done.

'Leaf thon pthams in the front hen,' the old woman said.

'Aye, aye. We will leave the prams in the front. That will save us taking them all up the stairs,' Dot smiled at the old dear.

We emptied the babies from the prams and made our way up the close excitedly. Charlie was bringing up the rear as usual and as I started climbing the close stairs he laughed. 'Thee you waiter then mitheth.'

Dot smacked him across the back of the head as he hurtled past her, causing him to bounce off the front door of the old couple's house. It made me laugh even louder.

'This is the smallest house I've ever seen,' Dot declared. 'How could it take you nearly two weeks to decorate this? If you stand in the middle of that kitchen you can touch both walls at the same time.' She tried to demonstrate her theory but was short by a foot.

'It's cosy and it's got its own wee bathroom. That's good, isn't it?' Darlene asked.

'It's not cosy Darlene. It's a house for munchkins,' Dot replied, shaking her head.

'Ah, but it's got high ceilings,' Tony declared.

Dot looked at him, 'That's great Tony. It's got high ceilings. So what do you suggest? That we put our furniture at the top of the walls? Maybe we could put wee Tony's cot on a pulley and bring him down when he needs fed or changed. How would that be?'

'Sounds brilliant,' Charlie said.

'I think she was being sarcastic Charlie,' I pointed out.

'Were you?' Tony asked Dot.

Dot didn't bother answering. She shook her head. It was Darlene who gave him a scathing look. 'Of course she was being sarcastic you halfwit. She's going to need the pulley to dry her washing.'

Dot looked at me. I shrugged my shoulders. Sometimes words are inadequate.

The front room wasn't much bigger than the kitchen. It had a bay window and a large recess at the back, which would hold a double bed with a bit of a squeeze. There was space in the centre of the room for a three-piece suite and a television, although it was so tight that you could reach the telly without getting up from the couch.

Dot was pleased that Tony had done the cleaning-up and decoration.

'Well Tony, it's not Buckingham Palace. But it's ours, and it gets us out from under their feet at my ma's. So let's get moved in tomorrow and we can make the best of it. It won't be forever. We can move on to something bigger later on.'

Tony put his arm around her and gave her a kiss: 'We will. I promise you Dot. We will be living in a big swanky house one day, with crystal chandeliers and paintings on the walls.'

Dot burst out laughing and kissed him back. 'Aye and marble statuettes as well, you eejit.'

31

'Well how was it?' my ma asked when we got home.

She was sitting in the kitchen with a cup of tea. Now and again she would wince but she seemed to be recovering quite nicely. There was still frostiness between her and my da. But when Dot and Tony moved out, and Dunky, Charlie and me moved into their room, it would only be Darlene in the living room. There would be nobody sleeping in the kitchen. That might reduce the stress levels.

'It's a wee doll's house,' Charlie said dismissively, opening the fridge and looking for something to eat.

'It was all right Ma. Tony's done his best to spruce it up. It is a bit wee. But it will be fine for the three of us,' Dot said, slapping Charlie as she passed.

'Dot, it's only been a few months since we were all in a room and kitchen in McLean Street. So maybe it's not as bad as you think,' my ma reminded her.

'No it isn't that bad Ma. I would have liked something a bit bigger. But it's ours and I can make it nice with my bits and pieces can't I? I'll be able to use all the wedding presents now. My nice dinner set from uncle Charlie and auntie Ina, and that continental-quilt thing from Tony's boss. He brought it back from London you know. I wonder what it's like to sleep under. It looks like a big pillow,' Dot said, cheering up at the thought of using her wedding presents.

'Oh I can't see that being any good. You'll be bloody freezing in the winter. No, you stick to a couple of good old grey army blankets and an eiderdown for when it's cold. Thae continental-quilt things won't be any good. Nobody will ever use them,' Donnie said, as he and Annie came into the kitchen.

Annie sighed. 'It doesn't matter what you put on the bed. At least you've got a house to put it in,' casting a resigned look at Donnie.

'I'm trying to find us a house. I've got my name down with the council, and with that chancer McCormack who rents out flats on the Paisley Road. What else can I do?' Donnie said petulantly.

'You can try a bit harder is what you can do,' my ma said. 'Annie needs her own house. It's all very well for men. Youse don't care as long as your tea's on the table and you've somewhere to put your head down. Youse would live in a cave if there was a telly in it for the football. But a woman needs her own house and her own kitchen. Annie won't tell you this, because she's trying to make the best of a bad lot. But I can tell you and I am telling you. Get your finger out and provide your wife with a house, the quicker the better,' my ma insisted, looking at Annie with a sympathetic smile.

'Aye, all right Ma. I'm doing my best. We're all right here for now,' Donnie replied.

'No, Donnie. *You're* all right here for just now. She isn't. No woman wants to live with her mother-in-law. I hated it and so does Annie. She's too nice a lassie to say it herself. But she does. So listen to what I'm saying and go get a bloody house,' my ma retorted, a little bit angry, both at Donnie's complacency and his unwillingness to listen.

'And you don't have to get a house round here. There are pubs everywhere if that's what you're worried about. Or you can get a bus to here if you really need to. Even Tony has managed to get a house so it canny be that bloody difficult. This might be all right for you. But it's not for her,' my ma added, with finality.

Tony didn't look too chuffed at the 'even Tony' part of her tirade. But he wisely kept his mouth shut. Annie, however, was pleased. My ma had said most of what she had been thinking.

Donnie had had enough. 'I canny walk into this bloody house without somebody moaning and nagging at me. No bloody wonder my da takes a drink. I'm off to the pub. And if I see anybody in the pub giving away houses I'll take one, okay.' He stormed out.

'God bless you hen. But you're gonny have your work cut out there,' my ma said to Annie with understanding written all over her face.

Dot grabbed Tony by the ear: 'It's not that bad Annie. Once you get them house trained they do what you tell them. They need a swift kick up the arse at times. But they're like puppies. If you give them a wee pet once in a while they get the message and do what you want them to do? Don't you Tony?'

'Woof, woof,' Tony barked, and then panted a couple of times. He caught Dot unawares and licked her face, jumping away before she could slap him.

Tony decided that he would join Donnie at the pub after getting Dot's permission and a handout of a couple of quid from her purse. Now that they were married what's his is theirs and what's hers is hers.

The three women then set about discussing ways and means of moving Dorothy out of my ma's house and into her own place.

'Will we need to top and tail your wee house Dorothy?' my ma asked, while putting wee Davie down in his pram for a sleep. Remarkably, all three babies were asleep at the same time, a minor miracle. Normally, when one was awake he, or she, woke up the other two.

'No, it doesn't look too bad Ma. I think when Tony was finished decorating his ma and his wee sister went along and gave it a good clean,' Dorothy answered.

'Well that surprises me,' my ma said. 'Looking at them at the wedding I wouldn't have thought they knew what a good clean was.'

Dot and Annie laughed, and Annie said, 'Oh that's terrible Maggie. You canny say that about them. Just because they had no fashion sense, and there were tidemarks round their necks. It doesn't mean they don't keep a clean house.' All three cackled this time.

'We will go along first thing tomorrow and give it a proper clean anyway Dorothy. You canny take a new wean into a dirty house. They catch everything that's going at the best of times. And you want everything spick and span before you put your furniture in. Well what furniture you've got,' my ma said, being practical.

'I've got my bed and my set of drawers. That's about it, for furniture. Tony's put a deposit on a three-piece suite in the second-hand shop at Govan Cross. I've got twelve pound to pay and that's it paid for,' Dorothy said.

'What bed and what set of drawers?' my ma asked, looking at Dorothy quizzically.

'The one's in my room of course,' Dot replied, puzzled by the question.

My ma came straight back. 'But if you take the bed out of that room where will Dunky sleep? The boys have got their bunk-beds but I was planning on Dunky going into that bed. And that would let Darlene sleep on the couch until such times as Annie and Donnie move out.'

'But that's my bed Ma. It's in my room. It's always been my bed and my set of drawers. I've never seen Dunky sleeping in it. Or any of his manky clothes in the drawers,' Dorothy replied, in a stroppy tone.

'Well I think your da will say different Dorothy. Because you slept in it doesn't make it yours. You didn't pay for it did you? No, your da paid for it. So I don't think he would be too happy if you helped yourself to a bed and drawers out of his house. He would need to go and buy new stuff. Why should he have to buy a bed and a set of drawers? If you think about it, I'm right,' my ma said, matching Dot's stroppiness.

'Where do you expect me to sleep then? On the floor?' Dot asked, getting angry.

'Don't be raising your voice to me madam,' my ma told her. 'You're married now. It's not up to me or your da to provide you with somewhere to sleep. That's up to your man. What did he sleep on at his house? Could you not take his bed?'

'He slept on a mattress on the floor. He pulled it out from under his brother's bed at night and pushed it back in the morning. We canny bloody sleep on that. How can I move into my house without a bed? This is ridiculous Ma. This isn't fair. I never counted on buying a bed, because I already had one,' Dot whinged.

'Will you be taking the washing machine and the telly as well? You use them so does that make them yours? By your reasoning you can help yourself to whatever you want as long as you used it the most,' my ma retorted, unwilling to back down.

I could feel the tension rising and did my best to ease it. 'Does that mean the kettle belongs to me because I'm the only one who uses it?'

They turned to me and said in unison, 'Shut up.'

Annie, on the other hand, covered her mouth to stop the laughter escaping. At least she appreciated my humour. Then, once she had controlled herself, she had a suggestion for Dot. 'Why don't you try Willie Brown's shop down at Kinning Park? He would do you a bed and a mattress on tick and let you pay it up. And his stuff is good and clean. He gets most of it out of houses where people have died. A lot of it is good stuff you know.'

'No way. I would never do that. Imagine sleeping in a dead person's bed. They would try to get in beside you at night. No way would I do that,' said Darlene.

'I think it would be brilliant,' was Charlie's opinion. 'You could get to know them and treat them as your own personal ghost and maybe train them to haunt other people, like sister or brothers.' He made what he supposed were ghost-like sounds and mimed an attack on Darlene.

'Will you all shut up? This is serious,' Dot began to say. Just as she started to say it we heard the toilet flushing.

My da came out of the bathroom and into the kitchen. 'Maggie, I've been thinking about what to do when Dot moves out. If she's taking her bed and that set of drawers with her, maybe I should have a word with Willie Brown about getting a bed and that on tick. He's not bad that way Willie. And it's good clean stuff he's got.'

Da couldn't work out why we were laughing so loudly.

The next evening we gathered at the close with carrier bags and boxes in our hands, waiting for Donnie to arrive. He had gone to get his mate who had a van and had offered to do Dot's flitting for a fiver. I say 'flitting' but, for all it was, it would only take half an hour. Donny arrived, not in a van, but with the horse and cart that had been used for our flitting. He looked like Harold Steptoe.

'Jesus Christ,' he said, jumping to the ground. 'This horse has been farting all the way from the Paisley Road toll and I'm sitting right behind its bahookey getting the full flavour.'

'At least it wasn't farting and then pulling the blankets over your head,' Annie said, poking her finger into Donnie's arm.

'I've no idea what you mean darling. And anyway, what have I told you about giving away our bedtime secrets?' Donnie laughed.

'How am I supposed to go on that bloody thing?' my ma wanted to know, pointing at the horse: 'Who do you think I am, Annie bloody Oakley?'

'You don't sit on the horse Ma. You sit on the seat behind it. There's room for two. Do you want to steer it Da?' Donnie asked.

'No you're all right son. I'm staying where I am. It doesn't take twelve of us to move a bed and a dozen bags and boxes. You can be the driver. I don't like the look of that nag.'

My da turned away before he could see the suspicious look my ma threw at him.

32

Donnie looked at my da to see if that was a deliberate dig at my ma and whether it would start the two of them off. But my ma didn't seem to be making much of the remark. So Donnie turned to the rest of us: 'Right, let's get everything loaded up. This horse and cart needs to go back before it gets dark or the horse will fall asleep where it stands.'

'That's no' true,' my ma said, 'John Wayne's horse doesn't fall asleep when he's chasing Indians all night.'

'Aye but John Wayne's horse isn't a lazy fat bastard from Bridgeton is it?' Donnie laughed, while tying the horse to the fence outside the close.

The cart was loaded up with everything that Dot and Tony possessed, including the bed and set of drawers that had been disputed. Mrs Wilson from the bottom close came out and asked Dot if she could use an old coffee table and a clothes drier she was getting rid of. Dot said 'aye' and they went on the cart as well. With all the boxes and bags, and Charlie, Darlene and I climbing on, it was like the *Beverly Hillbillies*.

Searcher obviously thought so because when he saw us from his window he shouted, 'Look everybody. It's the Cessnock Sillybillies.'

By this time my ma was agitated because the neighbours were at their windows, having a good nosey. 'Come on Donnie. That's everything. Let's get moving. All we're doing is putting on a show for the neighbours. You three hold on to something before you fall off and split your heads open.'

'It's all right Ma. If Charlie splits his head open we can use the mince that falls out for our dinner,' I joked.

Charlie fired back: 'It looks like Danny's head has already split open,' and pointed at the horse shit beside the cart. Everybody laughed, except me.

I'm not entirely sure how everything fitted into that wee house, but it did. Annie had stayed at home to mind the babies so when the unloading was done and Donnie said he was away to take the horse and cart back we thought he would go home and give her a hand. As it turned out, he didn't.

The first things unpacked were Dot's new electric kettle and the cups so Charlie and I were dispatched to the local shop for teabags, milk and sugar. I was given the honour of making the first pot of tea in Dot's new house. Lucky me.

Their belongings were moved into the house pretty sharpish and it didn't take long to empty the boxes and bags and put everything away. So it was quite early when we finished. As we were about to start the walk home, I noticed my ma and Dot having a wee cry in the kitchen. I didn't know why. Dot had moved into a new house and we had more space. What was there to cry about?

By the time we got back it was after ten. Annie was sitting in the kitchen.

'Where's my da and Donnie?' Darlene asked, at full volume as ever.

'Shush. I've just got wee Davie off to sleep, but this one is fighting it,' Annie whispered, looking down at the bundle in her arms. I presumed it was Mark. He was so tightly bundled it was impossible to tell.

'Paul went down an hour ago Maggie. He's in his cot in your room. So is big Davie. In your room, I mean, not in the cot,' she giggled.

'Where's Donnie and Dunky?' my ma asked.

'I was just going to ask you the same thing, I thought Donnie was with you lot. He's probably took that horse and cart back and stayed for a wee drink with big Jock. And I've not seen hide nor hair of Dunky all day. I think I heard him come in from work and go out again. That was just after you left to go to Dot's.'

'Well it wouldn't be a surprise if Donnie stayed for a drink with Jock. And I suppose Dunky will be chasing some lassie. You get yourself to bed if you like. I'll settle the wee yin down and then put him in his cot beside you,' my ma said.

'No Maggie, you're fine. I'm enjoying the peace and quiet. Couldn't half go a cup of tea but,' Annie said, winking at me.

It was four in the morning when I heard the three loud knocks at the door. It could mean only one thing.

The police were back.

What was Dunky up to now? It was a Wednesday night, so he couldn't have been at the dancing this time.

My da was first to the door with my ma right behind him, me right behind my ma and Darlene and Annie standing at their room door yawning, hair all over the place. Amazingly, Charlie was still sleeping, as were the three babies.

'Is there any need to chap so loud? There's weans sleeping in here,' my ma said in an angry whisper to PC Archie Brown, as my da opened the door.

'Well look who it is,' my da said. 'Archie Brown, back to have another go at the McCallisters. What can we do for you this time Archie?'

'You can turn up at the district court tomorrow morning at ten with a lawyer for your two boys, is what you can do. Or don't bother if you like. It's no skin off my nose. I would leave the toerags to rot if they were mine,' PC Brown answered smugly.

'What are they supposed to have done this time Archie? Been assaulting your fists with their faces again?' my ma asked sarcastically.

'No, Mrs McCallister. This time they have gone for the jackpot. This time it's breaking and entering, burglary and theft. And to top it off, the place they broke into was a police station.' He could barely contain his laughter.

My da shut the door before PC Brown could say any more, although we heard him laughing all the way down the stairs.

'Well, you will have to go tomorrow,' my da said to my ma. 'After all that bother last week, I will definitely get the sack if I don't turn up to my work.'

He was referring to the fight with his foreman in a pub the week before. This apparently hadn't been a sacking offence. In fact, it had made them friends, sort of. My da still thought the foreman was a halfwit but by not sacking him he had proved that he was 'just like us'.

So it was best to keep a low profile for a while and not take advantage of his better nature.

'It's just as well I'm not working. But how will I manage the weans?' my ma asked.

In Da's book, she was speaking a foreign language. 'Your weans, your problem,' he said, as he went back to bed.

'Aye they're always bloody mine when they're up to no good,' my ma sighed, following behind him.

As it was the school holidays I was taken to court with them so that I could sit outside with the babies. This meant that Annie and my ma could sort out a lawyer and find out what the score was. We got there just before ten, no thanks to Charlie and Darlene, who had both been acting up because I was going to the court and they were going to school.

'Why is he going with you? I always look after the weans but suddenly I'm not good enough. Well he can do it all the other times if he's so good at it,' Darlene sulked, holding her usual pose of crossed arms and petted lip.

'It's not about him being good at it. It's about you being off for two weeks while I was in hospital and the school threatening to take me to court. So shut up, get dressed and get to bloody school. What the hell would you want to go to a bloody court for anyway?' my ma shouted at Darlene. She was in a right fankle, trying to change David's nappy while Paul was hanging onto her knee, screaming for no reason.

Charlie being Charlie, unable to keep his mouth shut, asked petulantly: 'Why do I have to go to school? I went to school all the time you were in hospital. It's not fair. Why is it always him that gets everything and I get nothing?'

'What are you whingeing about?' Darlene screamed. What is he getting that you're not? That doesn't make sense. That's why you need to go to school and he doesn't because you're a wee idiot who canny even talk sense. And he should take you to school cos he's just as stupid as you. I am the one who should go with my ma and watch the weans.'

My ma exploded. 'Get to school. Get out of my sight both of you. As if I don't have enough on my plate without you two driving me up the bloody wall.'

A good result for me: Darlene and Charlie being screamed at and I get to miss school. Happy days or what?

It was pouring when we got to the court so Annie and my ma bumped the two big silver-cross prams all the way up the courts steps. Paul was strapped in at the bottom of wee David's pram with a harness. The harness had buckled straps, which attached to the sides. This meant that although the pram hood was on, the rain cover wasn't. So all the way up the stairs, while my ma bumped it up, I was holding a brolly over the pram trying to keep the weans dry.

When we got to the top of the steps there was a revolving door – Charlie would love this I thought – but it wasn't big enough to take the prams. There was a normal everyday door beside it, which could only be opened from the inside. So my ma gestured to a man in uniform to open the normal door. He shook his head.

My ma held her hands up, looked at the sky and said, 'It's bloody pouring. Open this door and let us in.'

The man came across and opened the door, but not to let us in. He stuck his head out. 'You can't bring prams in here. They're not allowed. You need to bring them in the door at the back.' He promptly shut the door in our faces.

'Bastard,' Annie muttered under her breath, as she bumped the big pram back down the stairs. The jobsworth was looking at us struggling back down the stairs and grinning smugly. Bastard right enough.

We eventually managed to get both prams to the bottom of the steps and around to a side entrance, where we were allowed in. A young lassie in a uniform told us to take the lift to the first floor. At the front desk we would be informed where Donnie and Dunky were and how we should go about finding a lawyer.

My ma said, 'Thanks hen,' then turned to me. 'You can stand here with the prams and we will be back as soon as we can.'

The young lassie in the uniform approached us. 'You can take the prams up in the lift. There's a canteen there where the boy can wait with the prams. They will heat a bottle up for the weans if you ask them.'

My ma put her hand on the lassie's arm, 'Thanks hen. Thanks very much.'

'What a bloody difference from that swine at the front door,'

Annie said. 'That lassie couldn't be more helpful, unlike that old bastard.'

As the lift doors opened we discovered that we were right opposite the revolving door where we had been a few minutes before, but this time on the inside. The old swine Annie referred to turned round and saw us emerging from the lift. He grinned like a cat that had got the cream.

Annie again muttered 'old bastard' and got ready to confront him.

My ma grabbed her arm and, loud enough for him to hear, said, 'Leave it hen. It's a bloody shame for the type of person that gets enjoyment out of somebody else's troubles. But everybody gets what they deserve in the end.'

The old swine obviously didn't agree because he was still grinning like a Cheshire cat when we walked past him to the reception desk.

I was put into the canteen with the three weans in their prams so I didn't hear what was being said at the desk. But I could see from Annie's attitude, and a fair bit of arm-waving and head-shaking, that things weren't going well. Then Annie went off with a guy in a black robe and my ma came in and sat with me.

'Annie's a bit upset,' I said, with a questioning tone.

She responded with an air of resignation. 'Aye well, that's her found a lawyer now. At first he told us,' indicating the elderly man in uniform at the reception desk, 'that Donnie and Dunky had been taken to Barlinnie this morning instead of here. Then he said that was wrong. They were going to be taken straight to Barlinnie from here, and then that was wrong as well. He then thought they had already appeared in court and had been sent to Barlinnie yesterday.

'In other words he had no more clue than we had where they were. Then that lawyer turned up and told Annie he was representing Donald and he needed a word with her. And here we are. Maybe he will know what's happening with Dunky. Go up to that counter and get two teas and a couple of caramel wafers. We can get Annie one when she gets back.'

We had finished our tea and I had eaten both caramel wafers before Annie returned. Remarkably, Dunky was with her. My ma got up, gave him a cuddle and slapped him on the face. 'What the hell have you been doing, breaking and entering? What the hell is that about?' she asked, trying to avoid alerting the other lost souls in the cafe.

Looking at them I don't imagine they were the least bit interested. They had their own troubles. There was a girl who looked younger than Dot – in fact she didn't look any more than fourteen – breast-feeding a baby. There was a toddler by her side. Her hair was matted and her skin was blotchy, possibly with crying. Periodically, she used the sleeve of her cardigan either to wipe away the snot under her nose or the tears leaking from her eyes. I don't know what her story was. Nor did I know the story of the old woman who went to empty tables and polished off leftovers.

'All right Ma. Take it easy. There was no breaking and entering or theft or anything like it. It's a load of shite,' Dunky said.

My ma slapped him on the back of the head again. 'Mind your bloody language,' she said, with a complete lack of irony. 'Of course you're gonny say it's a load of shite. But why are we sitting in a district court waiting for you and your brother if it's such a load of shite?'

Annie answered for him, which was probably just as well because the look on my ma's face told me that anything he said would result in him getting slapped again, and harder.

'Donald's taking the rap for it according to the lawyer. The procurator fiscal agreed to let Dunky go, if Donald pleaded guilty. The lawyer says that Donnie will probably get a fine because he hasn't got any previous convictions.'

'Well you can help him pay the fine,' my ma said, slapping Dunky across the back of the head for the third time. He put his hand up to protect himself but my ma, as always, was quicker on the draw.

We sat there for six hours before Donald was called into court. During that time the dregs of Glasgow paraded through the canteen. We saw everyone from homeless old men who smelled of shit to the shadiest barrow boys, who, even in a court canteen were trying to sell dodgy watches and what looked like half-bottles of whisky. Going by the spelling on the labels the 'whisky' was probably weed killer.

Dunky was going to buy a half bottle of 'The Famous Goose' before my ma told him not to be so bloody stupid and slapped him for the fourth time.

After three hours of waiting, Dunky started moaning. 'Why do we need to sit here all day Ma? Annie can wait for him and let us know what happened when she comes home. I'm starving and I'm no' paying for any more o' that muck they're selling in here.'

'Unbelievable, that's what you are Duncan. Bloody unbelievable. Your brother's in the cells under this court waiting to take the blame for something that was your fault and you're hungry and can't be bothered waiting for him. You're an ignorant, selfish, wee pig and always have been. I hope Donald slaps you one when he gets out,' my ma chided.

'It wasn't my fault. Was it?' Dunky whined.

My ma didn't answer. She looked at him as if he was an idiot. Earlier on – after Dunky had appeared and we found out Donald was taking the blame – Dunky told us what had happened.

33

The sorry saga had started the night before. After everything had been unloaded at Dot's new house Donnie was making his way back to Old Jock in Bridgeton with the horse and cart. When he got to the Viceroy bar at the toll he noticed Dunky standing outside talking to one John Boyd. He pulled the horse and cart over and asked Dunky if he wanted to come with him to Bridgeton, just for a laugh.

Dunky told him 'no' because it was a long walk back from Bridgeton and what would be funny about that.

As Donnie was about to leave, Johnnie Boyd shouted him back. 'I'll tell you what Donnie. I know how you could make yourself thirty quid with that horse and cart.'

Donnie looked sceptical but Dunky was interested. 'How? What do you mean thirty quid?' Dunky asked. 'What for?'

'For picking up scrap from a bit of spare ground and taking it to Langton's the scrappie in the Gorbals. I know where there's a load of lead and copper just waiting to be picked up,' Johnnie said.

Dunky was sceptical. 'That sounds too good to be true.'

'Well it probably is then. So get up on the cart and come with me to Bridgeton,' Donnie butted in. Dunky jumped up on to the seat beside Donnie.

But Johnnie wasn't beaten yet. 'Wait, wait boys. Don't look a gift horse in the mouth. Ha ha. Do you get it?' he chortled, pointing at the horse. 'Look, I'll show you where the stuff is and if it's not kosher you gallop off into the sunset. You've got nothing to lose. And if it is kosher, and you make a few quid, you slip me a fiver tomorrow night. Job done. Bob's your uncle.'

Which sounded reasonable enough, except that none of the three of them understood one simple fact: if you find something of value you can't just keep it. That's the law in Scotland. It's theft by finding. If you find something you need to hand it in to the police station and if no one claims it within a set period of time it becomes yours. But even without that awareness they should have known that lead and copper attached to a building wasn't 'waiting to be picked up'.

Thinking about theft by finding, I wonder what happened to that wee lassie I saw at the back of the Sherbrooke hotel. The one who said she had found that big bundle of fivers, and was going to buy shoes. I wonder how she got on.

When they reached the Gorbals, Seaward Street to be precise, Johnnie Boyd pointed out a derelict building, 'There you go. Look at all that lead lying about.'

He was correct. A fair bit of lead sheeting had been stripped off the roof. It was on the ground at the side of the building, but there was three times as much still on the roof.

'Look up there Donnie, at the gable end,' Dunky said, pointing at two massive copper sheets that would be worth a right few quid as scrap. Along with the lead, Johnnie was very close with his estimate of thirty quid. In fact, it was probably more.

Donald had made up his mind. 'Fuck it. Let's go for it.'

As he and Dunky walked towards the boarded-up door, Johnnie Boyd called out: 'Okay then lads. See you tomorrow with my fiver then.'

'What are you talking about? Come and give us a hand or you can dance for your fiver,' Dunky said.

'I don't think so Dunky boy. I told you I would show you where it was. And do I look like a fuckin' navvy?' Johnnie asked.

They looked at him standing there in his old black trousers and a torn jumper and spoke with one voice: 'Aye, you do,' they laughed.

Johnnie looked down at himself. 'Well all right. You've got a point. But I'm not a worker. I'm a tell-people-what-to-do sort of guy. So get on with it and bring my fiver tomorrow as agreed. Tally-ho chaps,' he called out as he walked away.

My brothers set about their task with relish and within ninety minutes they had the cart fully loaded with lead and copper. There was so much that Donnie was afraid the old nag wouldn't be able to pull the cart. Unfortunately, they had an audience for the last half an hour of their toil: PC Archie Brown and PC Agnes McFadyen. The latter looked a bit like PC Brown, except more manly.

'Well well Donnie. Somebody's been working hard. That's a right good pile of scrap you've got there. I bet it's worth a few quid,' Brown said, with his usual smugness.

Donnie wasn't daft. He knew they were in a tight spot.

Dunky, however, didn't realise the gravity of the situation. 'Aye and it's took us well over an hour to get it all off Mr Brown. But it will be worth it when we get it to Langton's.'

'Aye son. You certainly look to have worked up a fair old sweat,' McFadyen smiled.

Dunky wasn't sure how to take this. It seemed like she was flirting. She was a polis and pot ugly into the bargain. But she was still a woman so maybe the best thing would be to flirt back. You never knew. It couldn't do any harm.

Thirty seconds later they were both in the back of a polis van, under arrest for breaking and entering, theft and burglary. McFadyen also wanted Dunky charged with lewd and libidinous behaviour because he had said to her: 'How's about a gander under that uniform doll? We can check out each other's truncheons if you like.' To her way of thinking, this wasn't flirting.

So that's how we got there. And that's why we had been waiting for six hours for Donnie to appear in court. The lawyer Annie had spoken to earlier on turned up at four and told us: 'Right that's him being brought up in front of the sheriff. His case is being heard in court five if you want to run along there.'

My ma and Annie jumped up and my ma said, 'You two watch the weans until we come back. Dunky, if you bugger off before I come back I'll be telling your da, and he will sort you out.'

'All right Ma, all right. I'm not going anywhere. It shouldn't be that long anyway,' Dunky said, with a modicum of contrition.

After they had left, a weasely looking character came across to our table and sat beside me and opposite Dunky. He brusquely pushed one of the prams aside as he sat down. 'Hey watch what you're doing pal,' I said. I wasn't being brave. Dunky was sitting right next to me.

The weasel ignored me and said to Dunky: 'Well, I see they let you out. Did you do what I told you?'

Dunky looked uncomfortable: 'No, Donnie took the rap. His lawyer said he would only get a fine.'

The weasel sat back in his seat. He looked at me and said, 'See that wee man. You give somebody good advice and they haven't the sense to take it. Listen Dunky, my boy,' he said, putting his hand on Dunky's arm. Dunky pulled away with obvious distaste, as if the guy was wiping something on him.

'Listen Dunky. You brother's probably going to the Bar L now. If you had said it was all down to you, it would have been the children's panel and a kick up the arse at worst. It's Sheriff Longmuir in court five and he hates thieves. He always gives them time. You're a couple of dafties right enough. You didn't listen to your wee pal, King Rat, so you deserve all you get. Ta ta for now.' That said, he got up and weaved away to another table.

'What's he all about, King Rat?' I asked Dunky.

'He's from Pollok. His name is Dennis King. There was a guy in a book called King Rat who knew everything about prison and could get you anything. So this prick calls himself King Rat and thinks he knows everything. He knows fuck all. But he is a wee rat.'

I smiled but it froze on my face when I saw Annie coming towards us. She was crying and my ma was right behind her, looking furious.

'Forty-five days, forty-five bloody days in Barlinnie. For picking up some old scrap. You pair of bloody eejits. That's him had it now. His job will be away. There's no chance of him finding a house if he's in the bloody jail. And look at her. She's beside herself. She's left with a newborn baby and not a penny to her name. I could bloody throttle the pair of you,' my ma shouted at Dunky, grabbing him by the collar and shaking him.

Annie stood there, weeping uncontrollably.